WHY DID I
LOSE
MY JOB

if God loves me?

• HELP AND HOPE DURING CAREER TRANSITION •

RICK J. PRITIKIN

ZONDERVAN®

13 14 15 16 17 18 19 20 21 /DCI/ 23 22 21 20 19 18 17 16 15 14 13 12 11 10 9 8 7 6 5 4 3 2 1

To my daughters — Diane, Lauren and Bethany.

You girls are my life!
I pray your children will be
as much of a blessing to you
as you have been to me.

TABLE OF CONTENTS

ACKNOWLEDGMENTS

I must first mention my dearest friend, a wonderful Christian lady and official prodder — Layne Cagle. You are the best! Thanks to the guys at the Career Transition Support Group in Brentwood, Tennessee — Matt, Rick, Hal, Dave, Don, Ed and all of the volunteer speakers. For 23 years, this great group has given hope, education and encouragement to thousands of graduates!

Chuck Sugar, there would be no Christian Fellowship & Placement Ministries without you. You are a great brother and friend. David Sutton, you provided a much-needed Samson in my life, in addition to many meals. I love you, Bro! Dave Dixon, you are a true friend and brother. Your support kept the ministry and me going, and your prodding helped to make this book a reality.

Bobby D aka Bob DeMoss, you are a trusted friend, dear brother in Christ and much more than just a catalyst. The Lord has richly gifted you, brother.

A special thanks to Amy Ballor, my development editor at Zondervan. You have the patience of a saint. Thank you for all of your efforts to bring this devotional book to market.

And to each person who reads this and sees a bit more sunshine on a gloomy day: The Lord's timing is *always* longer than we hope, but *never* late ...

AUTHOR'S NOTE

It was 10:30 a.m. on April 26, 2003. The closing on my new house was scheduled for 1 p.m., and I had one more thing to wrap up at the office — a quarterly review of my work as a senior-level executive. I figured the review should take about 30 minutes and then I'd be on my way with bonus in hand. Or so I thought. Instead, at 11:30 I was calling my mortgage banker to ask if they were in the practice of making loans to people out of work. Fortunately, I was able to get out of the deal.

That's when my career transition journey began. With little warning, I joined the millions of people who were in a place they may have never been before — struggling to find a job.

According to the United States Bureau of Labor Statistics, as of this writing, the unemployment rate stagnated for the third straight week at 8.2 percent. That represents over 12.5 million men and women dealing with the roller coaster of emotions and fears known as career transition. In addition to the 12.5 million people in transition who are actively seeking a new career position, there are an additional 5.4 million who have been unemployed for more than 27 weeks and have given up believing that a job is available for them.

More than simply statistics, these are real people — neighbors, friends, family members. And since you've picked up this book, you may be in the same boat.

Speaking from firsthand experience, the impact of unemployment can include depression, financial turmoil, marriage and family difficulties, increased sensitivity, anxiety and low self-worth. When we're in transition, shame is often at an all-time high while encouragement is at an all-time low.

After months of doors closing in my face and my children asking that dreaded question, "Dad, when are you going to get a job?" several events — including two major offers from two large companies falling apart at the last minute within a few days of each other — determined a new path for my life.

One Sunday while sitting in church and processing my unemployed status, I began to look around the congregation. I realized that I knew several business owners in the audience. Some of them were likely in need of employees and might be dreading the task of placing ads and having to sort through hundreds or even thousands of résumés.

I reasoned that some of them may even have to make a decision the next morning to hire or fire someone. Many of them must be praying for wisdom and guidance for the tasks ahead. Many were praying for a Christian to fill the open positions. I wondered why I didn't know about any of the positions. Surely, one of these employers could use someone with my talents.

At the same time, I thought that many of the men and women in the congregation must be in the same position I was in. In fact, there were probably hundreds who either needed a job, hated their job or were working extra part-time jobs just to make ends meet. Why didn't all of them know about the opportunities represented in this auditorium?

Then the question came: How do we bring together these employers with these men and women? What better way to strengthen the church, build the community and seek to achieve the "city on a hill" Jesus speaks about in Matthew 5:14? There had to be a way. That's when I received a vision for a ministry that would accomplish this in our church.

My dear friend and Christian brother, Chuck Sugar, got tired of hearing me talk about the need for a ministry to bring these groups together and challenged me to just do it. With his help, we did it. We created a business plan for Christian Fellowship & Placement Ministries, which became my passion and calling but not a full-time, paying job. Chuck and Randy Trigg, who caught the vision early on, continue to be a mentors, supporters and cheerleaders.

Soon after the ministry was founded, we began having meetings to encourage those in career transition. The response was tremendous. This was the only place many people could find spiritual and emotional encouragement specific to their needs. We also had a desire to involve spouses, children and other family members.

Most of the men and women were filled with despair because of their circumstances. I knew the Lord had taken me on my journey so that I could relate to their feelings, needs, disappointment, anger and depression. I felt completely inadequate, however. How could I help them when I was in need of so much help myself?

I began meeting one-on-one with men and women in every stage of career transition and every stage of family and marital disharmony resulting from a lack of income. The common denominator continually seemed to point to a lack of self-respect, self-esteem and self-confidence.

The letters and calls of appreciation for restored hope and improved relationships began to roll in. I realized that a meeting every other week wasn't enough to encourage these people in a way that would last 14 days. One day during my devotions, the Lord placed on my heart a verse that gave me hope. I felt compelled to share it with the others in transition. Since I didn't want to wait until the next meeting, I sent an email to everyone who was on the ministry roster. I included the verse and a few thoughts about how I felt it related to my transition journey.

The reaction was nothing short of amazing. I received dozens of responses from people telling me how that verse had spoken to them in their situation. That motivated me to write this devotional. You'll notice it is designed in a format that allows you to take notes and journal your thoughts. You can choose whether to share your reflections with your loved ones or allow this to be your special space where you can be totally honest about your feelings, concerns and fears.

My prayer is that you will read each devotion several times, coming back to them again over time. Each time I believe you'll find a new message, a new perspective, a new opportunity to see you are not alone, and a new attitude that will help you through the transition journey. The Holy Spirit will talk to you if you listen, and encouragement will follow.

I also encourage you to find one special person with whom you are able to connect and share your deepest concerns and feelings, as well as begin to communicate more with your spouse, children and other loved ones so they better understand your journey and what may be expected of them along the way. *This is not the time to cocoon!* This is the time to accept the help of loved ones, friends, networking groups, your church family, your pastor and especially God through prayer. I know you will find prayer to be a real comfort.

One final thought. When your transition journey is over (yes, it will end) and you are in that new career the Lord has for you, don't forget those who helped you. Pay it forward. Get involved in a local career group, or start one if none are available. Check with your state's closest career counseling center to see what resources are available and where you may offer assistance. Be available to those you know are who are in transition. Offer to meet with them. Never forget what you needed.

I pray that in some small way the pages that follow will bless you with peace and a closer relationship with the Lord.

— RICK PRITIKIN

In my distress I called to the Lᴏʀᴅ; I cried to my God for help. From his temple he heard my voice; my cry came before him, into his ears. —PSALM 18:6

"It just can't get any worse."

How many times have you caught yourself saying this during your career transition? For me, it has been more times than I care to admit. And if I'm completely candid, my very next line is usually, "How much more, Lord? How much longer must I wait for a breakthrough?"

I often wonder why the Lord doesn't just reveal to me exactly where he wants me to be. He has the power to do anything and everything, right? So why can't he just show me? Maybe the reason for this mystery is so that we will turn to him. After all, what do we need the Lord for if we already know what will happen?

I, for one, find myself neglecting my Bible reading and prayer time when my career journey is humming along on all cylinders. I simply don't spend time with the Lord every day as I should. When things are hitting bottom, however, I guarantee that I will seek the Lord's presence. Now the reason I seek God might be to blame him for my circumstances. I might cry out, "If you love me, why did I lose my job?" or "How much longer must I wait until I can provide for my family again?"

To be honest, my comments often are not civil in tone. But guess what? God is not fragile. God will not run from the room with his hands covering his ears so that he doesn't have to listen to me as I vent my frustrations and disappointments.

Do you know what's great about all of this?

God already knows what you and I are feeling! The Lord knows me better than I know myself. He knew, before I was even conceived, that this painful season of my life was going to take place; he knew exactly what was going to happen to me and exactly how I was going to react. He also knew that unless I fell upon the worst of circumstances I would not grow closer to him.

Let me put it to you this way. Have you noticed the times when you are closest to the Lord? Isn't it when all else has failed and you are driven to cry out to your loving heavenly Father? Now imagine if those tough times had not occurred.

Your relationship with him might be less intimate than it is today. That's why we are in the best position to grow closer to God when we are experiencing the perceived worst of circumstances.

He *does* know what is best for each one of us. Sometimes he just needs to get our attention so he is able to bless us beyond our greatest expectations. Why not give the Lord your fullest attention today by setting aside the job search for a while and spending some uninterrupted time with him? Just listen. Be still. And if the message doesn't come through today, he may be saying, "Not yet. There is more I want to show you."

If that's his message, why not invest more time with him again tomorrow? Why? Because some things are more important than a job — like intimacy with the One who holds your life in his capable hands.

POINTS TO PONDER:

Trials are part of the human condition. Can you name a time in your life when the Lord put you through a trial that was not ultimately for your good? Make a list of the trials you've experienced in the past, and then describe how he used those difficult times to provide for you, to stretch and strengthen you, or to open doors you didn't even know existed.

_____

_____

_____

_____

_____

_____

_____

_____

_____

_____

_____

_____

_____

_____

_____

_____

_____

_____

_____

_____

_____

_____

_____

_____

HELP WANTED:

Heavenly Father, I come to you with fear in my heart, and yet I know you are aware of this and all my other doubts. Help me to lean on you, dear Father. Help me to desire to be closer to you in these times of trial. Calm my soul; help me to allow the Holy Spirit to enter my heart and the glory of your presence to engulf me. In Jesus' mighty name I pray. Amen and Amen.

Consider it pure joy, my brothers and sisters, whenever you face trials of many kinds, because you know that the testing of your faith produces perseverance. Let perseverance finish its work so that you may be mature and complete, not lacking anything. —JAMES 1:2–4

I'm often asked what I consider to be the toughest part of the career transition journey. I usually reply with "How much time do you have?" But the truthful answer for me is that the toughest part of the journey has been learning more about myself than I was ready to accept. That seems to be a universal response. Most of us would be just fine without knowing how much fear we really harbor within ourselves, how low our self-esteem really is, or how much our previous job, with all its perks, formulated our net worth as a person.

A number of years ago I lost my job. In that difficult season, which lasted the better part of two years, I kept hidden from myself my concerns, my indecision, my anxiety and my lack of sincere faith in God as my ultimate provider. I didn't even have the faith of a mustard seed. I was reminded of Jesus' words, "Truly I tell you, if you have faith as small as a mustard seed, you can say to this mountain, 'Move from here to there,' and it will move. Nothing will be impossible for you" (Matthew 17:20). But in *my* version of the passage at the time, the mountain laughed at me and said, "Loser! Get a job, and maybe then I'll listen to you!"

Yes, the toughest part of the journey was coming to terms with the person I had become — a man whose faith had been weather-beaten. It was having to wake up every morning to face that person in the mirror I was not even sure I knew anymore — the fragile person who could be brought to tears by a mere question from my children about our vacation plans. I was no longer Mr. Confident. I was easily shaken over a budget-busting electric bill. I suffered deep feelings of despair when a form rejection letter regarding a job opportunity I thought I had in the bag arrived in the mail.

Only when I came to the end of myself did I become humble enough to face the real me — and my real God. Much to my surprise, in the midst of this desert experience I came to accept the blessings of life; I learned to slow down enough to savor the beauty of creation. I actually smelled my first rose in years, and I thanked God for allowing me another breath and another day of life (see also Psalm 8). I gazed at the leaves on the trees — and then stepped back to really *look* at the trees! I took my first deliberate look at the stars at night, and in the midst of that peace and wonder I marveled at the magnitude of the heavens and the hands of the One who flung the galaxies into space.

And for the first time in a long time I had conversations with my children in which I actually paid attention.

I still had worries, but in this unhurried season I felt a peace that the Lord would provide for my needs — a peace "which transcends all understanding" (Philippians 4:7). The real me still questioned, still feared, still hurt and, yes, still cried. But I discovered at my core that I know my God is real and he knows what is best for me. I know that when a door closes, I'm not being punished, but protected. And I know that when the perfect door does open, I will be better prepared to enter it than I was when this journey began.

What is the toughest part of the transition journey? The toughest part is making your way to the very bottom of self — so that you can truly enjoy the blessings of comfort, love, contentment and joy that only your heavenly Father can provide. My prayer is that you too will embrace the toughest part of the journey so that you may experience the best part of life now, as well as when he provides that new career opportunity.

POINTS TO PONDER:

During your transition journey, what has the Lord revealed to you about yourself, your lifestyle and your needs that you had not allowed yourself to be aware of when money was available and a job defined you?

_____

_____

_____

_____

_____

_____

_____

_____

_____

_____

_____

_____

_____

_____

_____

_____

_____

HELP WANTED:

Dear Lord Jesus, I know you desire the best for me as one of your children. I acknowledge that you have placed these trials in my path to make me go deeper in my relationship with you and to trust in your hand of provision. Help me to draw comfort from the fact that even as you provide for the birds and the fields, you will always be with me. In Jesus' mighty name I pray. Amen and Amen.

TRANSFORMATION HAPPENS

Therefore, I urge you, brothers and sisters, in view of God's mercy, to offer your bodies as a living sacrifice, holy and pleasing to God— this is your true and proper worship. Do not conform to the pattern of this world, but be transformed by the renewing of your mind. Then you will be able to test and approve what God's will is— his good, pleasing and perfect will.
—ROMANS 12:1–2

Oswald Chambers, the early twentieth-century Scottish minister and author of the classic devotional *My Utmost for His Highest*, once observed, "Grapes become wine only when they have been squeezed." I know a thing or two about being squeezed. In fact, when I was going through a seemingly endless, two-year career transition without work, I expanded Chamber's adage: *The best wine comes from grapes that have been squeezed the hardest.* There is something in this analogy of being squeezed and transformed from the common grape into a costly vintage wine that is instructive in our discussion about career transitions.

For instance, during my extended unemployment I was tempted to think that being without a job was the worst thing that could happen to me as a provider. I've since learned that having a job but no perspective — or having a perspective that's out of balance — is much worse. Believe it or not, I came to thank God for the four areas of radical transformation that took place in my life while I was without work. Allow me to unpack those insights, as I'm convinced you will likely see yourself in my mirror.

First, without the busyness of a daily grind, I was able to see with clarity how my entire life was driven by my work. My identity, my self-respect, my self-esteem and my sense of self-worth were all centered around my occupation. I was an executive, first and foremost. Not a dad, not a friend, not a volunteer and, to be honest, not a happy person. Once my job was no longer in the picture, I was able to attain a more healthy balance. In turn, I developed a much brighter outlook on life.

Second, without the job pressures chasing me home every day, I began the process of detoxing. I had no idea how stressed out I had become literally every waking minute. I was a bundle of nerves. I was stressed about work, about life, about career, about family issues, about children issues. I was on, if you will, a "double shot" of anxiety medication just to keep from getting anxiety attacks from the stress! Several months without my responsibilities as an executive, however, transformed me into a much calmer frame of mind. In fact, the transformation in my inner man was noticeable to those who knew me before and after I lost that job. They even asked me how I was so calm when things were in such disarray in my life. Clearly, the "peace of God, which transcends all understanding" (Philippians 4:7) was able to take root once the anxiety of performing on the job was squeezed out of me.

The third transformation that took place was physical. I was in such bad shape that I was like a walking pharmacy. I was on so many prescription drugs that my copay every month was over $800. I had high blood pressure and high cholesterol, and I was always tired. Upon exertion, I experienced swelling of the ankles and chest pain. Guess what? During the first year of being without work, with the reduction in my stress level my blood pressure returned to normal, my cholesterol dropped more than 100 points to the low range, and I reduced my dependency on medications by 50 percent.

Perhaps the most significant difference was the growth in intimacy that I experienced with the Lord. I spent more time with the Bible than ever before. I became more active in men's prayer groups and mentoring opportunities, becoming more accountable than at any time in my life. I had never felt so secure in my salvation or in the security of knowing I could pick up the phone at any time and receive encouragement and counsel from someone who really cared about me.

Are you being squeezed today? Are you feeling pressed in from all sides? Is that process producing only pain, or are you seeing the seeds of transformation taking root? Are you asking the question, If God loves me, why did I lose my job? Take a moment to list the blessings you have right now, instead of dwelling on the things you no longer possess — and watch for the transformation that is sure to come!

POINTS TO PONDER:

Whether you have been in transition for a day, a week, a month, a year or longer, do you see transformation taking place in the midst of the squeezing? What changes in your outlook do you see? In your physical health? In your stress level? In your realization of, and thankfulness for, your blessings? In your time with the Lord? If you don't feel some of the positive results I experienced, consider whether or not you are truly committing yourself to the Lord — and if not, try it!

_____

_____

_____

_____

_____

_____

_____

_____

_____

_____

_____

_____

_____

_____

_____

_____

_____

_____

_____

_____

_____

_____

_____

_____

_____

_____

_____

_____

_____

_____

_____

HELP WANTED:

Dear Lord, I pray for continued "squeezing." I pray that you will continue to reveal to me the many positive things you have been doing in my life. I pray I will continue to turn everything over to you, knowing that you are faithful to your Word. I am thankful for your endless love and for your fulfillment of the many blessings I enjoy every day. In Jesus' name I pray. Amen and Amen.

**Peter replied, "Even if all fall away on account of you, I never will."
"Truly I tell you," Jesus answered, "this very night, before the rooster crows,
you will disown me three times." —MATTHEW 26:33–34**

Are you discouraged today because, in spite of your best efforts, you can't seem to land a job interview? Are you wrestling with feelings of despair because full-time work continues to evade you? Has your spouse or another family member wounded you with their words because you're unable to provide as you once did? Are you tempted to deny that God still cares for you because somehow you've blown it?

Let me unpack this two ways: with a personal illustration and with Peter's story.

When I was 12 years old, I made the all-star team in the Chicago Baseball Little League. I'll never forget one big game against a nearby league. I came up to bat in the bottom of the last inning; the score was tied, there were two outs, and the bases were loaded. I was shaking all over as I approached the plate.

The coach had told me to take the first four pitches. Four pitches? I could strike out without even swinging the bat.

The first two pitches were way outside. The next two were strikes. My coach called me over and said, "Take one more pitch, and then you're on your own."

The next pitch missed the strike zone, so now the count was full. The pressure was unbelievable, as I realized this was a defining moment for me and for my team. I knew I could get a hit if I just kept my eye on the ball. I waited for the pitch. The ball had to be at least two feet outside. I swung … and missed. I would have sent the ball into the next county if my bat had only been several feet longer!

As I approached the dugout, the three guys who were stranded on base followed me in, saying, "Nice going, Rick. You just blew the game for the whole team!" Wow, did that hurt.

The game went into extra innings — and we lost. Even though I went on to bat .500 in post-season play, it seemed like I was never able to make up for my failure in their eyes.

The hurt and despair of being unemployed while in the "big leagues" of life, especially with a family to provide for, was far more devastating, since the consequences are greater than losing a ballgame. We're talking a loss of career, a loss of income, a loss of self-respect and a loss of identity. What's more, if we allow our emotions to go unchecked, failure in our career path has a way of leading to depression — especially the longer our job search drags on.

If anyone in the Bible had a reason to be crushed by despair it would have been Peter, a disciple of Jesus. Just before Jesus' arrest, Peter arrogantly proclaimed that he would never leave or betray Jesus — even though Jesus had just predicted that all of his disciples would fall away. Jesus, in turn, assured Peter that he would indeed deny him before the rooster crowed three times. And sure enough, Peter did.

Listen to the intensity of Peter's denial in Matthew 26:74: "Then he began to call down curses, and he swore to them, 'I don't know the man!'"

He called down curses? This was no casual denial or "innocent" white lie. After the rooster crowed, we're told, "Then Peter remembered the word Jesus had spoken ... And he went outside and wept bitterly" (Matthew 26:75).

But that's not the end of Peter's story. Peter had a choice to make. He could fall into utter despair and accomplish nothing, or he could find his strength in Jesus to carry on — which is what he chose to do. This illustrates that even Jesus' disciples messed up, yet they got up and continued on their assigned path.

Is our transition journey so very different? I think not. We fight despair. We wrestle with the debilitating thoughts and feelings that no one wants our talents. We even toy with the idea of giving up on God's ability to provide for us.

Let me encourage you to *get up*! Your journey is not over. In fact, it may have just begun. With the Lord's help we must get up from our self-pity, our sea of regrets and our fear of failure, and proceed to the next opportunity. Don't allow anything to come between you and the assigned task the Lord has for you.

POINTS TO PONDER:

Admitting that we've rejected the Lord during our career transition takes courage. Has despair and self-doubt caused you to think that God is no longer on your side? If so, reflect on how you've allowed self-pity to replace your trust in Jesus, and resolve to turn that around.

Compare Deuteronomy 31:6 – 8 and Psalm 37:25 with Revelation 2:4. What do they have to say about God's faithfulness to his people?

_____

_____

_____

_____

_____

_____

_____

_____

_____

_____

_____

_____

_____

_____

_____

_____

_____

_____

_____

_____

_____

_____

_____

_____

_____

_____

_____

_____

_____

_____

_____

_____

_____

HELP WANTED:

Heavenly Father, I confess I have rejected your love for me more than three times. I am lower than Peter. And yet I know you have not given up on me (and will not) even when I have given up on myself. I ask you to lift the veil of despair that has clouded my vision and prevents me from seeing your hand at work in the midst of my career transition. In your mighty name I pray. Amen and Amen.

ACTIVITY OR PRODUCTIVITY?

**My son, do not let wisdom and understanding out of your sight,
preserve sound judgment and discretion. —PROVERBS 3:21**

If you haven't read the book *Who Moved My Cheese?* by Dr. Spencer Johnson, I suggest you do so — as soon as possible. Dr. Johnson offers this insightful parable about mice and humans and how each of them deals with change. As is the case with all allegories, symbolism is used to drive home the point. In this story, the mice and the humans represent various personalities. These pages will certainly help you get a clearer perspective on how you are handling — or not handling — your career transition. Perhaps you will see some of yourself in this parable, as I did.

Without giving away too much of the story, allow me to offer a snapshot. During a period of change, the humans in the story work very hard on a project that yields no results. They continue to work hard at it — while the project continues to yield no results. At one point the realization sets in that there is a difference between *activity* and *productivity*.

That simple observation hit home with me early on in my career transition. I confess I spent days filling out forms and answering questions on every website I could find that would allow me to connect with potential employers. I even found websites for jobs that I would never consider taking — but I didn't hesitate to fill out the forms!

Somehow I had convinced myself that I was really working hard on getting another job. And so I worked for hours upon hours, day after day. Like the humans in *Who Moved My Cheese?* I finally realized that I was wasting my time. I'm not saying that all of the websites were bad; I'm just saying that I realized I was kidding myself by thinking that I was being productive when all I was really being was active. There's a *big* difference.

That was not the end of my learning curve. I thought I had learned my lesson and wouldn't make that mistake again. Wrong! A partner and I launched a business to sell "stuff" on the Internet. I spent days creating forms, form letters, return authorizations, fancy descriptions and the like. In spite of my activity, the business failed miserably. Yet I was sure we just needed different product descriptions, better camera shots, different days when the products were featured — you get the picture.

Even though I knew what the outcome was going to be after the first week, we kept this charade going for over two months. I tried to convince myself (and, candidly, my family and friends) that I was really busy trying hard to make a new company grow. The reality? I was trying to convince myself that I was being *productive* when I knew in my heart that I was just being *active*.

Is it time for you to accept the fact that your "cheese" has been moved? Is it time for you to stop convincing yourself you are being productive, when you know you are just filling time with activities? Proverbs 3:21 encourages us to preserve "sound judgment and discretion." I view those characteristics as the two "missile keys" that can launch a more realistic assessment of whether what we're doing is just being active or really being productive in the pursuit of full-time work.

After all, sound judgment and discretion allow us to stand back and be clearheaded about the stewardship of our time, the value of a particular networking opportunity, or the worth of engaging in a particular activity, such as filling out on-line applications. They also prompt us to seek God's wisdom throughout our career transition rather than relying on our own efforts, which can so easily be misguided.

Why not start your journey from *activity* to *productivity* today? Spend some time this week plotting out your new course — using the sound judgment and discretion that God freely offers you to direct your steps.

POINTS TO PONDER:

Which is easier for you: filling out a job application on-line, or meeting with a recruiter in person? Why? What specific steps might you take today to make at least one real-life connection in your field of interest?

_____

_____

_____

_____

_____

_____

_____

_____

_____

_____

_____

_____

_____

_____

_____

_____

_____

_____

_____

_____

HELP WANTED:

Dear Father, I confess my tendency to fill my life with all sorts of things that occupy my time but fail to be truly productive. Please convict me when I'm doing things just to be active, and give me the courage and vision to be truly productive. I trust you to guide my steps. In the name of Jesus, Amen.

He withdrew about a stone's throw beyond them, knelt down and prayed, "Father, if you are willing, take this cup from me; yet not my will, but yours be done." —LUKE 22:41–42

Any minute an armed mob would burst into the Garden of Gethsemane and arrest Jesus. The one through whom "all things were created" (Colossians 1:16) was within hours of laying down his life to pay the price for the sins of the human race. So we find Jesus that fateful night. Alone. Praying. Weeping.

For you. For me.

Jesus had the power to do anything he wanted to do. He didn't have to endure the spitting, beating and verbal insults dished out by his tormentors. In the flash of a moment, every person who abused him could have been dust. Yet Jesus obeyed his Father, completed the journey he was destined to make, and paid the ultimate price for sins he never committed. What's more, he did it all without complaining.

I have wondered what I would do if I had been in some of the situations our Lord encountered. If someone spit in my face, what are the odds that I would still love them? If someone was mocking and beating me, what are the chances I would turn the other cheek? If my hands and feet were nailed to a cross while my earthly possessions were divided by the executioners in front of me, would I maintain a heart of compassion for them? Never! And yet that was the "cup" Jesus knew he would have to drink in order to complete his work on earth.

By contrast, if you're like me, you've been in situations where you lost your temper at the slightest infraction — such as shouting in disgust because another driver didn't use their turn signal or took "your" parking spot at the market. You might get bent out of shape over small things like a restaurant server neglecting to refill your water or your coffee. These situations are embarrassingly trivial compared to what Jesus endured. Yet nothing dissuaded our Lord from his journey to the cross. And in his case he knew what was going to happen before it happened!

So here I sit typing these words on my laptop while sipping on Diet Coke —

with a bright light over my head, running water ready when needed, food in the refrigerator, clothes on my back, a car outside my home and money in my pocket. What's more, I'm blessed with good health, three great daughters, one terrific grandson and brothers and sisters in the Lord who truly love me. But what do I do? I complain because God hasn't shown me what my next career opportunity will be.

Let me tell you, right this very second I am ashamed. Not because I may possess a bit more than the next person, but because I'm impatient with the process of finding something more meaningful to pursue. I want the cup to be taken from me. And I am too self-absorbed to realize I am blessed beyond description — since Jesus took the cup and fulfilled his journey, paying the price so I can rest in his arms forevermore.

I just need to obey God's Word: "Wait for the Lord; be strong and take heart and wait for the Lord" (Psalm 27:14).

Whether you're unemployed, underemployed or looking for a new profession, don't be discouraged by the current state of your career. The Lord will walk with you through your journey. He will be with you every step of the way — even carrying you if necessary.

After all, Jesus went to the cross for you and me. He isn't about to give up on us now.

POINTS TO PONDER:

What causes you shame during this journey? Embarrassment that you lost your job when some people you worked with for years stayed on? Insensitive words from a frustrated spouse who has just about given up on you? List all of the factors and situations that bring you shame. Then reflect on the fact that your Savior bore your shame on the cross so that you no longer need to carry that burden.

_____

_____

_____

_____

_____

_____

_____

_____

_____

_____

_____

_____

_____

_____

_____

_____

HELP WANTED:

Dear Jesus, what a blessing you are to me. What a Savior! I am not only saved, but I also don't have to worry about my ultimate destination. In you I have hope. How, then, can I be so self-absorbed? How, then, can fear darken my path? Help me to remember that fear has no hold over me, for you walk with me and carry me when I am weary. In your holy name I pray. Amen and Amen.

GLORIFY HIM

Teach us to number our days, that we may gain a heart of wisdom ...
May the favor of the Lord our God rest on us; establish the work of our hands
for us — yes, establish the work of our hands. —PSALM 90:12,17

Anytime I speak to an audience of job seekers and quote Psalm 90:17, inevitably someone will corner me afterward and say something like, "Rick, I am ready to have the Lord establish the work of my hands. I am *more* than ready. In fact, I am *beyond* ready. Sometimes I just don't get it. What is he waiting for?"

I understand that sentiment. When I was unemployed for an extended period of time, I wanted to know how much longer I had to trek along this transition journey until God showed me the work my hands should be establishing.

That's when I discovered an important message in Psalm 90. This psalm reminds us that our days are numbered. We don't know how many days we've been given on this earth — maybe many, maybe few. This is why God's Word admonishes us to be good stewards of whatever time we have, to use each day to "gain a heart of wisdom." I have come to see that this translates into doing all we can for the Lord and for his kingdom.

Allow me to paraphrase something Rick Warren, author of *The Purpose Driven Life*, has said: God has placed us here for a purpose and that purpose is to glorify himself. Not for us to glorify ourselves, but to glorify him. That perspective changes our priorities. No longer should our focus be on concerns like where the rent is going to come from, how the credit card bill will get paid, or how we will be able to afford the car payment. While we do need to act responsibly, our larger focus should be on what we can do today that will glorify the Lord, and on what job opportunity would allow us to serve him best and to advance his kingdom.

As the Westminster Catechism famously states, "Man's chief end is to glorify God, and enjoy Him forever." Yet if I'm completely honest, I must confess I have lived most of my life trying to glorify myself in the eyes of other people. My greatest desires were to create wealth, acquire stuff and spoil my children. I accomplished all of my goals, to a certain degree, but unfortunately none of those accomplishments were the ones the Lord had in mind for my life. I used my time to build my little kingdom on earth while leaving a few spare minutes now and then for him. That's where the words of Psalm 90 convict me. I've not always been a wise steward of my time. Furthermore, since I was created to glorify God and enjoy him, why don't I start acting like it?

Those in career transition might not feel like glorifying God right now. They might feel, instead, that they deserve a pass. I know I did. After all, isn't it his fault that we are in this position? He could have changed the circumstances and we would still be employed.

Yes, our situation could have been different, meaning that we wouldn't have to wrestle with anxiety and anger. Can we be expected to glorify God by trusting him in the midst of this crisis? Yes. I believe the Lord sometimes uses trials to sharpen our focus in order to realign our priorities according to his will.

I encourage you to take some time right now to examine where you are. What are you doing with the days the Lord is granting you? Are your days just passing by, or are your hands busy doing things that will bring him glory?

The worst thing possible would be to forget that God has a purpose for our lives — a purpose that will advance his kingdom. If we get real close to him, I believe he will remind us of that plan and purpose.

POINTS TO PONDER:

Fear, which is a by-product of the transition journey, can keep us from being wise stewards of our time. The question is, What will you do with your fear? Make a list of everything you are afraid of. Are you afraid you may never find a job? Are you afraid of losing your home because you can't pay the rent or mortgage?

Now pray over your list. Ask God to help you discover his higher purpose for your life in whatever career he will ultimately reveal.

_____

_____

_____

_____

_____

_____

_____

_____

_____

_____

_____

_____

_____

_____

_____

_____

_____

_____

_____

_____

_____

HELP WANTED:

Heavenly Father, you know that I harbor feelings of anger toward you. I blame you for my problems. Yet I confess that I haven't been using my days to seek first your kingdom. Help me, Jesus, to desire to be so close to you that I will hear your whispers of direction. I pray for your perfect love to quiet my fears on this journey. In your holy name I pray. Amen and Amen.

HE WILL LIFT YOU UP

**"God opposes the proud but shows favor to the humble."
Submit yourselves, then, to God. Resist the devil, and he will flee from you.
Come near to God and he will come near to you. Wash your hands,
you sinners, and purify your hearts, you double-minded ... Humble
yourselves before the Lord, and he will lift you up. —JAMES 4:6–8,10**

Humility. What an uncomfortable word — not to mention a word that I knew
very little about before my transition journey began. Dictionaries define humility
as having a modest opinion or estimate of our own importance or rank. On the
flip side, I admit that if you looked up the word *arrogant* in the dictionary several
years ago, it could have displayed a picture of me with a smug-looking smile on
my face. I was at the top of my game and at the top of my field. But I had lost
sight of the fact that any modicum of success I might enjoy is a by-product of the
blessing of the hand of God.

Psalm 75:7 puts it this way, "It is God who judges: He brings one down, he
exalts another." Indeed, I learned that the hard way when God, because of his love
for me, humbled me by reducing my little self-made kingdom to rubble.

James says we are to humble ourselves "before the Lord" — which, if we're honest, is as uncomfortable as it is foreign to the self-made, pull-yourself-up-by-your-
bootstraps man or woman pursuing a career in "a dog-eat-dog world where only
the strongest survive." After all, on the surface humility doesn't fit into the pursuit
of success in the workplace.

I'm reminded of a line from Frank Sinatra's classic song, "My Way." In it, "Ol'
Blue Eyes" croons how he lived his life on *his* terms, a man who says "the things
he truly feels and not the words of one who kneels." Clearly, there is no room for
humility in Sinatra's worldview.

I mean no disrespect to "The Chairman of the Board." For far too many years,
I embraced Sinatra's mantra. However, James tells us that there's a better way to
conduct our affairs. In fact, those who choose to practice humility in the presence
of God will be lifted up by the hand of God. What a wonderful promise!

I'll be the first to admit that a career transition is a time of tough decisions, insecurity, low self-esteem, doubt and having more questions than answers. It is also a time when our humility and integrity will experience its greatest challenge. We can either build up ourselves to appear larger than life, or we can be humble, honest and transparent about our difficult circumstances. I've known people in transition who have maxed out their credit cards in order to maintain an illusion that all was well — while the termites of debt and financial disaster were eating away the foundation beneath them. They refused to sell the fancy car and drive something more modest. They held on to their boat when their finances were sinking. And they paid their monthly mortgage by juggling a string of credit cards rather than downsizing their home.

Which road are you going to take today — the path of pride or the path of humility?

Are you tempted to forsake humility in order to enjoy acceptance by others? Are you sacrificing your testimony and an opportunity to develop a closer walk with the Lord during your season of career transition just to impress someone? Are you going to allow pride to get in the way of what the Lord has waiting for you if you humble yourself before him?

I pray that you and I will be ever-watchful to resist the devil when he tempts us to be prideful and lie about our journey and our needs. Why? Because those who humble themselves before the Lord *will* be lifted up. That's a promise straight from the heart of God.

POINTS TO PONDER:

When someone asks how you are doing, how do you typically respond? Are you transparent about your brokenness? Do you ask others to pray for a breakthrough in your job pursuit?

Have you turned down a certain line of work because you felt it was beneath you? What might you learn about humility and the heart of God if you were to take a position that required a cut in pay and status?

_____

_____

_____

_____

_____

_____

_____

_____

_____

_____

_____

_____

_____

_____

_____

HELP WANTED:

Dear Lord, I know all things are possible through you. And I know that all too often I listen to the devil rather than to you. I pray for humility and for honesty — with you and with myself. If my focus is on you, I know the devil will have no chance to distract me with his lies. Give me strength as only you can. In your precious name I pray. Amen and Amen.

Very early in the morning, while it was still dark,
Jesus got up, left the house and went off to a solitary place,
where he prayed. —MARK 1:35

I often hear people in career transition make pious-sounding statements like "You know, Rick, I'm looking for the Lord's leading in my life"; or "I'm waiting on the Lord for his perfect direction"; or "When the Lord has the right job for me, he will let me know." Another familiar refrain is "Why hasn't God spoken to me yet, Rick?"; or "Why hasn't the Lord shown me where he wants me to be?" I believe these individuals are sincere when they express these feelings. Yet far too often I get the sense they're only being partially honest about their quest for God's leading.

Not known for mincing words, I'll reply with something like, "You say you are seeking to hear from the Lord. But when was the last time you spent an extended time in quiet seclusion so you are able to hear him when he speaks? I don't mean rushing through your daily Bible reading. I mean quality time alone with God for more than thirty minutes. What about more than one or two hours? How about four or more hours?"

Don't get me wrong. I'm not a spiritual superhero who flies through the pages of Scripture with the greatest of ease. I admit that I struggle to carve out much time for protracted prayer and Bible study. But isn't that the behavior Jesus himself modeled?

Mark reports that "while it was still dark," our Savior had a habit of heading to a "solitary place, where he prayed" (Mark 1:35). Evidently Jesus felt the need to fellowship with his heavenly Father in an undistracted setting. In like fashion, for you and me to hear where the Lord is leading us in our journey, to have the ability to commune with him without interruptions, we must get away from the "noise" of our lives, with its endless eye candy and diversions.

This is easier said than done. Almost anywhere you go these days there are televisions cackling away in a corner. From the TVs in our homes, to the multiple

TV screens hanging from ceilings in restaurants, to the TV in our pockets on our cell phones, it's difficult to escape the constant stream of entertainment. Nevertheless, we have this example of Jesus who went to a solitary place to hear from God.

Elsewhere Mark notes, "After leaving them, he went up on a mountainside to pray" (Mark 6:46). Luke writes, "Jesus often withdrew to lonely places and prayed" (Luke 5:16). What's more, sometimes Jesus "spent the night praying to God" (Luke 6:12). Are you seeing a pattern here? Our Elder Brother wisely leveraged quiet places to hear from God the Father and fellowship with him.

I'm not necessarily suggesting that we have to leave our homes in order to experience solitude — although retreating to the mountains, a state park or a beachside cottage would be a wonderful way to leave behind the noise of this world. That's not always practical, however. But the isolation necessary to hear from God can exist wherever you are physically. How? By turning off your cell phone, television, radio and any other electronic device that might break your focus.

You might also consider spending time outside, especially during the dark of night or the predawn morning hours. A local park or preserve offers a great place to sit and meditate on the Lord. This time is best spent alone — no spouse, children or friends; no phone contact; no texting. Although the noise of civilization may be around you, such a setting will be much more quiet than your normal routine.

"He Is Not Silent," a song by Out of the Grey, summarizes our situation: "He is not silent. We are not listening." Do you really want to experience the Lord's leading in your career transition? Then recognize that none of us will ever know what his direction is until we nurture a closer relationship with him.

POINTS TO PONDER:

When was the last time you spent an extended period of time fellowshiping with the Lord? Where can you go to find a place of seclusion to hear from him? Make a list of potential places and try them out.

Reflect on Psalm 119:105. See how much clearer your pathway will be when you hear his voice.

_____

_____

_____

_____

_____

_____

_____

_____

_____

_____

_____

_____

_____

_____

_____

_____

_____

_____

_____

HELP WANTED:

Dear Lord, I realize my need for solitude — for a place of privacy where I can meet with you. I so desperately need to hear from you. Help me, Father, to seek your face and to yearn for your company more than the distractions of my daily life. I ask you to direct my journey and to give me the calm spirit that I so desire. In your holy name I pray. Amen and Amen.

> **"For I know the plans I have for you," declares the L**ORD**,**
> **"plans to prosper you and not to harm you,**
> **plans to give you hope and a future."**—JEREMIAH 29:11

While I'm not exactly a trivia junkie, I've always been intrigued by odd facts and bits of information. For example, if I were to ask you which of the more than 31,000 verses in the Bible is the most popular, what would you guess? I'll give you a hint: It's the verse you often see on placards at football games. That's right — John 3:16. "For God so loved the world that he gave his one and only Son, that whoever believes in him shall not perish but have eternal life."

How do we know that's the most popular verse in the Bible? The folks at BibleGateway.com have the ability to tally the most frequently searched Scripture references on their website. Not long ago they listed the top one hundred verses based on twenty-five million Bible passage searches over a two-month period. Scanning the list, I noticed that Jeremiah 29:11 came in second place: "'For I know the plans I have for you,' declares the LORD, 'plans to prosper you and not to harm you, plans to give you hope and a future.'"

Did you notice how many times the word *plans* appears in that verse? Go ahead, count them. I was struck by the intentionality of the Lord to give us "hope and a future." After all, a plan speaks of design, of forethought, of establishing a goal and an outcome. I believe it's fair to say that God is revealing something about his character — that he is a loving, gracious heavenly Father who has our best interest in the center of his heart — while also modeling for us the virtue of having a master plan.

How appropriate for the focus of today's reflection — namely, developing a "game plan" to manage your career transition. As I see it, if having and executing a plan to reach a desired outcome is modeled by God, then the process of crafting a plan of action to navigate a career transition ought to be important to me. In short, a game plan means proactively scheduling our time to achieve results. Without a plan, we flounder and wander aimlessly, with little progress to show for our activity by the end of the day or the end of the week.

Celebrated NFL football coach and NASCAR team owner, Joe Gibbs, puts it this way: "A win in football starts with a game plan. In racing it starts with a race plan. The same goes for life. You want to win? You need a winning game plan. My experience has taught me that the only winning game plan for life is God's game plan — and it starts with the Bible."[1]

This is why you'll notice that the first thing on the following seven-part game plan I created involves the Scriptures.

1. I will start each day with at least seven minutes of Bible and/or devotional reading and prayer. (Feel free to increase this amount as soon as you are in the habit).
2. I will meet with my spouse or roommate every week to update them on what I have been doing and on my job-search plans for the next week.
3. I will select a companion with whom I can be totally honest and accountable, and meet with them weekly. (This should not be the person in point two.)
4. I will set up at least one networking appointment each day and/or make a minimum of ten calls per day pertaining to my job search.
5. I will attend at least one meeting pertaining to job skills per week at a local career center.
6. I will spend at least two hours per week doing volunteer work, such as with a church, mission, ministry or nursing home.
7. I will review and adjust my game plan on a weekly basis.

This is just a starting place. Whether you use my game plan or create your own, remember the words of Proverbs 16:3: "Commit to the LORD whatever you do, and he will establish your plans."

POINTS TO PONDER:

Read Proverbs 15:22. Why do our plans fail, and what is necessary for them to succeed? Who are the people in your life who are having a positive impact on

---

1 Joe Gibbs, *NIV Game Plan for Life Bible* (Grand Rapids: Zondervan, 2012), viii.

your career journey? Make a list of those you would trust with your deepest feelings, and then ask one of them to be your accountability partner (if you don't have one already). Also identify those who could serve as a mentor if there are areas where you know you could use some improvement.

_____

_____

_____

_____

_____

_____

_____

_____

_____

_____

_____

_____

_____

_____

_____

_____

_____

_____

_____

_____

_____

_____

_____

_____

_____

_____

_____

_____

_____

HELP WANTED:

Dear Lord, I come to you recognizing that you have a plan for my life, that you desire to give me hope and a future. I yearn for your hope to fill my heart today. Give me courage and wisdom to design a game plan that will help me reach my goals and will protect me from stagnation and mediocrity during this transition. In your mighty name I pray. Amen and Amen.

THE LORD FIXED MY REFRIGERATOR

**I will give thanks to you, Lord, with all my heart;
I will tell of all your wonderful deeds. I will be glad and rejoice in you;
I will sing the praises of your name, O Most High.** —PSALM 9:1–2

When you read the book of Psalms, do you find yourself resonating with the psalmist's gratitude? Do you find yourself giving thanks to the Lord with all your heart? Are you quick to think about all of the blessings you have? Do you feel like singing praises to God? Or is giving thanks and praise to the Lord more "complicated" when you are without work?

When I had been without work for about a year, I remember reading Psalm 9 in my devotions and having a really difficult time being thankful for my circumstances. This psalm forced me to search my heart and dig deep regarding what I really believe about God. Is he worthy of my praise and thanksgiving only when things are going my way? Will I stop telling others about his blessings just because I had a temporary career setback?

I confess I had more of Job's wife than Job in me. Remember their exchange in the book of Job? Job was a wealthy man who lost everything in two blinks of an eye: his livestock, servants and children one day and his physical well-being another day. Covered with painful sores from head to toe, Job's suffering was so intense that his wife's counsel was to "curse God and die!" Job, however, replied, "Shall we accept good from God, and not trouble?" (Job 2:9 – 10).

Like I said, my response leans toward the attitude of Job's wife. I certainly don't give thanks to the Lord in the midst of my predicaments. I tend to be much quicker to remind God of what I don't have or of what I have lost.

When we lose our means of providing, we face some tremendous tests of our character, such as remaining positive in the face of bills that are due, staying upbeat while forgoing items that we can no longer afford, or retaining a thankful heart even when we have to cancel the vacation we had been looking forward to before we lost our job.

What's more, when we aren't sure where the money is going to come from, we're forced to turn to the Lord and rely on him — a cycle of dependency and trust that's a bit absurd when you think about it. Why do we turn to the Lord when we're at the end of our ability to control a situation? The fact is, you and I are *never* in control of *any* situation. Without the Lord, our abilities and actions are never going to solve the problem. When will we maintain our faith in the Lord regardless of our circumstances?

Allow me to illustrate a healthier response, demonstrated by a friend who was excited to share one of those Psalm 9:1 "wonderful deeds" of the Lord with me. His refrigerator had broken down; and being unemployed, he didn't have the money to buy a new one. Rather than freaking out or complaining, that night he prayed for the Lord to fix his refrigerator. Yes, he actually prayed that! Now I don't know about you, but of all the things I have requested of the Lord, refrigerator repair has never come to mind.

The next morning my friend discovered ice cubes in the freezer compartment, which hadn't worked at all the day before. The day before, he had turned the temperature setting all the way down to try to get the last few cool gasps out of the appliance and moved all the food to the lowest shelves of the refrigerator to try to take advantage of whatever small amount of refrigeration might be left. He checked the food and found that it was starting to freeze! The Lord had heard his prayer, and he couldn't wait to share the good news with me.

Oh that our hearts would maintain a posture of thanks, trust and praise regardless of our circumstances.

POINTS TO PONDER:

Is giving thanks in all things easy, somewhat difficult or impossible for you? Why? Are you preoccupied with the question, *When will the right job come along?*

_____

_____

_____

_____

_____

_____

_____

_____

_____

_____

_____

_____

_____

_____

HELP WANTED:

Dear Lord Jesus, I want my heart to be filled with gratitude for you and for all you do for me. I pray for a thankful heart when I don't feel thankful. I pray for your Spirit to engulf me and replace all doubt and uncertainty. I pray I will always see the good in what you have done and continue to do in my life. I pray for faith in all things and for the desire to accept your answer even when it's not the answer I'm looking for. In your holy name I pray. Amen and Amen.

**As soon as Jesus was baptized, he went up out of the water.
At that moment heaven was opened, and he saw the Spirit of God
descending like a dove and alighting on him. And a voice from heaven said,
"This is my Son, whom I love; with him I am well pleased."**
—MATTHEW 3:16–17

You may be reading this during the heat of summer, the dead of winter or the rains of spring. I believe the insights will be applicable regardless of the season you're in. I happen to be writing with Christmas around the corner and "Jingle Bells" ringing in my ears. In fact, this evening I attended a children's Christmas program at church. While I had no children in the program, for reasons I can't explain I found myself reflecting upon a difficult Christmas season when I was without work and how I desperately wanted to lavish gifts on my children that year.

After all, while I had been employed the presents for my three daughters almost filled the entire family room. But the year I lost my job, I knew holidays like Christmas would be different — radically different if measured against a roomful of gifts and trash bags overflowing with the remnants of unveiled surprises. As difficult as this was for me to embrace, I discovered that while a career transition may mean fewer store-bought gifts, I could offer more tangible demonstrations of love and oneness of family spirit. My home became a place of being thankful for what we had rather than yearning for what we did not receive.

The fact that I didn't have a job didn't change the longing in my heart to do everything I could do to make Christmas special for my children and grandson. I was happy to sacrifice as needed — even foregoing some of my own presents to ensure they would have as much as possible. After all, we parents will do everything in our power to shower love upon our children. Sacrifice is synonymous with parenting; that's just the way it is. If you're a parent, do you remember the utter joy you felt when your children were born? From that moment, I knew there would be little else in life that could bring such joy — and that there would be no sacrifice too great for my children.

While I was having these reflections during the Christmas program, it dawned on me that our heavenly Father must have felt immeasurable joy at the sight of his Son being born in Bethlehem. What's more, the Lord was delighted as his Son grew and was baptized. In fact, God spoke from heaven, saying he was "well pleased" with Jesus. And yet, Father God, because of his love for you and for me, willingly made the ultimate sacrifice of his Son Jesus on the cross.

Here's the connection to your job search. Would God — who loves you so much that he sent his Son to earth to live, die and be raised from the dead on your behalf — somehow forsake you during your career transition? You might want to reread that. And do you realize that today, right now, God is well pleased with you too? That's why he sent his Son in the first place! I hope you sense him wrapping his loving arms around you and calling to you. I pray you will respond with trust and faith in him both now while you're in your career transition as well as once you've come to your journey's end.

POINTS TO PONDER:

What have you had to sacrifice during this career transition journey? How important were those things to you? How have you shown others that your relationship with Jesus has more than replaced the things you may no longer have?

_____

_____

_____

_____

_____

_____

_____

_____

_____

_____

_____

_____

_____

_____

_____

_____

_____

_____

_____

_____

_____

HELP WANTED:

Dear Lord Jesus, as I reflect upon the sacrifice you have made for me, I am brought to my knees. I am humbled and ashamed, as I know you cry for me when I don't really believe what you endured for me. Help me, Father, to see you in all my frustrations during this transition journey. Help me to be grateful for what I have — for nothing is more precious, more beautiful or more needed than my relationship with you. Help me to be a living testimony to my family and friends of your agape love. In your holy name I pray. Amen and Amen.

LIVE LIKE CHILDREN

[Jesus] said: "Truly I tell you, unless you change and become like little children, you will never enter the kingdom of heaven." —MATTHEW 18:3

Do you sometimes wonder if God has forgotten you? Do you wonder if he's too busy to keep track of the details of your life? Are you holding on to the notion that you lost your job because God is mad at you or he wants to punish you? Do you think he's so swamped with requests that there is no way he would want to be bothered by your prayers?

If I may be direct, these questions reveal something deficient about our view of God. Think about it. Jesus could have said that we needed to change and become like a trusted citizen, or a faithful soldier, or a devoted servant/employee. No, he desires us to become like *children*.

The apostle John wrote, "See what great love the Father has lavished on us, that we should be called children of God! And that is what we are!" (1 John 3:1). Since you and I are his children, doesn't it stand to reason that God desires to guide our paths in all things — including our search for a job? Wouldn't he want the best for us? And wouldn't our "*Abba* Father" (see Romans 8:15) communicate his guidance to us?

After all, such behavior is consistent with what any loving earthly parent would do. This begs a difficult question. How can we hear from God if we're not daily seeking his direction? Don't rush by that question, it's an important one. Furthermore, why should we expect the Lord to lead us and guide us on the path he has for us if we're not actively seeking his input?

Let me put this into perspective with an illustration. As any parent can attest, raising children involves a constant desire to teach them and to prepare them for the future. Likewise, parents desire to protect their children from making bad decisions that only age, wisdom and experience teaches. Even when our children resist and don't want to listen, we still try to get through to them.

When our kids are young, they require constant vigilance, attention and communication. As they grow older, contact between parent and child oftentimes slips into a pattern of less contact with Dad and Mom as other things occupy their time. Of course, when there's a crisis, you and I get the call, right? When our children have no one else to turn to, or when they come to realize that they don't have the understanding or experience to handle a particular situation, it's time to call Dad, it's time to ask Mom. They know they will receive comfort, guidance, direction and love. While their communicating with us and their seeking our advice may be after the fact, and while we may be the last resort, they have confidence that we will be there for them.

And just as I allow my children to follow their path without demanding my input, the Lord doesn't force me to come to him. He allows my free will to have its way. Clearly the Lord desires that you and I, as his children, would come to him sooner rather than as the last resort — just as I wish the same for my children.

Matthew 18:3 tells us that we are to come to the Lord like *little* children, which suggests dependency on our part and guidance on his part. That should have special meaning for you as you face the issues in your career search. Not that we should act like children, but that we should seek understanding, guidance, knowledge and comfort from his Word, with the trust and expectancy that little children have when approaching their parents.

Do you believe the Lord is your answer when things get tough? Do you really believe he has a plan for your career search and for your life? If so, don't you agree you need to be checking in with him on a daily basis? Why not make today the beginning of a daily discussion with the only One who really knows you?

POINTS TO PONDER:

What obstacles have you encountered that could have been easier if you had been praying about them? How much time are you spending in the Bible on a daily basis? Do you typically attempt to live life, and conduct your career affairs, in your own strength? How would your life be different if you approached the Lord like a "little child"? Why not try seeking your Abba?

_____

_____

_____

_____

_____

_____

_____

_____

_____

_____

_____

_____

HELP WANTED:

I cry out to you, Abba, Father. I am in need of your comfort as my "Parent," my "Daddy." I know you allow me to make my own mistakes. You are patient with me when I neglect your leading. But I am ready now to listen. I know that being closer to you will provide the constant assurance and comfort I need. I realize that my way is not the answer I need; it is your way that will guide me through this journey and help me to find true peace and comfort. In your holy name I pray. Amen and Amen.

WHEN WILL YOU GET IT?

**"Come to me, all you who are weary and burdened,
and I will give you rest. Take my yoke upon you and learn from me,
for I am gentle and humble in heart, and you will find rest
for your souls." —MATTHEW 11:28–29**

My three beautiful, wonderful daughters have been and continue to be a tremendous blessing to me. During their formative years, however, I often forgot what a blessing they were and instead found them to be a bother, a burden, a distraction from what I wanted to be doing. I know that sounds horrible, but it is true. The Lord knows I would give anything to return to those years and be more present in their lives, rather than being consumed by my career desires.

All three of my daughters really struggled with math. When they were younger, I was our family's designated math teacher for homework. No matter how many times I would review their geometry, division or multiplication lessons, I heard the same objection: "I just don't get it." The tutoring sessions would usually last about five or ten minutes before all three girls were in tears. I couldn't understand why they were unable to grasp the concepts when I had reviewed the material with them so many times. I finally got the message through "back channels" (via their mom) that I needed to be more compassionate of their plight.

When I reflect on my past career transition journey, there were definitely times when I thought my heavenly Father must have been as frustrated teaching me as I was instructing my daughters. I imagined him saying, *My son, how much longer will it be before you get it? What will it take for you to follow my lead instead of making your own path? Why won't you learn from me?* You see, the temptation is to think that we will be able to resolve our career transition mess on our own somehow, when in reality finding a job is all in God's perfect timing and in his perfect plan for our lives.

While there are similarities between my learning from my heavenly Father and my daughters learning from me, there's one huge difference: My Teacher never gives up. In fact, rather than pushing me away in his impatience, he says, "Come to me." Although I may be in tears, my Teacher comforts me and never berates me when I fail to get it. Instead, he sees me, holds me and says, "I love you; please try it my way."

Do you feel as though someone is standing over you, telling you how you have been doing it all wrong? Are you straining under a burden of stress, thinking you must be all messed up since you don't have a new opportunity yet? Are you the one who ends up in tears and feels the frustration of not knowing how to get it?

If so, why not take a moment right now to thank your heavenly Father that he is a patient, long-suffering teacher? Why not turn your quest for work over to him and spend more time with him each day so that you can more easily hear the right answers? Jesus promises those who submit to his "yoke" that they "will find rest for [their] souls."

POINTS TO PONDER:

Think of the times when it was all you and your abilities that got you where you were. Now think of the times when you really felt that the Holy Spirit was leading and empowering you. When did things work out better?

_____

_____

_____

_____

_____

_____

_____

_____

_____

_____

_____

_____

_____

_____

_____

_____

_____

_____

_____

_____

_____

_____

_____

_____

_____

HELP WANTED:

Heavenly Father, I need to be refreshed in the knowledge and understanding that only you can truly direct my paths to meet my goals. I am reminded that you alone are the One who comforts me in my time of sorrow, wiping my tears dry. I pray that I will be more open to your Holy Spirit and seek you in all I strive for, rather than trying to get by on my own understanding and efforts. I pray this in your holy name. Amen and Amen.

**Cast all your anxiety on him because
he cares for you.** — 1 PETER 5:7

I have a hunch. I wouldn't be surprised if you were to say to me, "Rick, one of the problems I struggle with is an inability to enjoy what is happening right now. For some reason I am always looking ahead and just don't get the joy of the *now*." Sound familiar?

I resonate with that sentiment. Here is a perfect example. Prior to my transition journey, I would take my two younger daughters on vacation. We always planned a fun getaway to a very nice destination. In the weeks and days leading up to the vacation, however, I was planning and worrying about how we would get to the airport, when we would have to leave, how we would keep track of the luggage, etc. On the way to the airport I would wonder if I had forgotten to lock the back door at home.

Unlike their worrywart father, my girls were excited. They asked questions about where we were going and what we would be doing while preparing for a terrific family time. I confess I was absent emotionally from sharing in their joy and in their anticipation and discussions because I was too hung up on the details of planning the next step. To make matters worse, when we arrived at our destination I started worrying about making sure we got the luggage and the right transportation to the hotel.

When we arrived at the hotel, I was planning the trip to the pool while unpacking the luggage, and wondering who should get a key to the room. When we got to the pool, I was planning the order for showers afterwards and where we would have dinner. When we got to the restaurant, I was planning how to get back to the hotel or how late I should let the girls stay up. You get the idea.

It was only after an event that I realized that I really didn't remember much about it. Even today my girls will say, "Dad, remember when we were in California and such and such happened?" I would have absolutely no recollection of the event at all. I was too busy worrying about or planning the next step, instead of enjoying the moment. Today I think of all the joy I have missed that can never be replaced.

Here's the connection to your transition journey. If you allow anxiety to drive your thoughts, all the blessings you have received will be lost in the worrying about where the next month's rent will come from or how you will manage to put gas in your car. My friend, whether you go on a vacation or, due to a lack of funds, you have a "stay-cation," those family memories cannot be relived. They will be gone if you let them. The joy that could have been and should have been will be lost.

What about your journey? Are you focused on tomorrow, next week or next month? Are you planning for the "What ifs" instead of focusing on the right now? First Peter 5:7 reminds us to cast *all* our anxiety on the Lord. What does that do? It takes the pressure off us and places it on his able shoulders. After all, the prophet Isaiah assures us that God "will be the sure foundation for your times, a rich store of salvation and wisdom and knowledge; the fear of the LORD is the key to this treasure" (Isaiah 33:6).

Isn't that great news? The Lord will carry our burden for us, and he provides from his storehouse of wisdom what we need to know to get through this minute. If you are traveling on this career journey worrying about tomorrow, isn't it time to stop and smell the roses? Take some time and look for the blessings you are receiving, the friendships you are making and the answers to prayers you are receiving.

Remember, our heavenly Father loves us unconditionally and wants the very best for us. How can we possibly know how wonderful a life he is providing if we don't start living in and enjoying this moment?

POINTS TO PONDER:

What events or moments have you missed during your journey? What blessings of family, friends or opportunities have you allowed to pass by because you were too worried about tomorrow or the mortgage that is due next month? List these events and blessings. Then ask the Lord to help you enjoy the journey from here on out!

_____

_____

_____

_____

_____

_____

_____

_____

_____

_____

_____

_____

_____

HELP WANTED:

Heavenly Father, help me to see you in my everyday life. Help me to enjoy each moment in this journey rather than worrying about tomorrow. Help me to rest in your Word's instruction that worry is a burden you never meant for me to bear. Help me to be present by focusing on today. May I let tomorrow be tomorrow and next month be next month. In your mighty name I pray. Amen and Amen.

Those he predestined, he also called; those he called, he also justified; those he justified, he also glorified. What, then, shall we say in response to these things? If God is for us, who can be against us? He who did not spare his own Son, but gave him up for us all—how will he not also, along with him, graciously give us all things? —ROMANS 8:30–32

You might want to take a moment and read that passage again. As you reread those three verses, ponder these questions: What did God give up for you, and what else is promised to you?

If we are open to the Holy Spirit, every time we read God's Word we very well could receive new insights. Does this Scripture make you feel like you could do anything with God in your corner? When I considered these verses recently, the words just made me feel like an eagle — empowered to soar above it all. Why? Because God is on my side. If God would sacrifice his own Son for me, what *wouldn't* he do for me?

Here is where I believe the message gets a bit difficult to understand for those who are without work, without the daily purpose that comes with a job and the means to provide. In fact, I imagine these verses at times seem to offer a mixed message from the Lord. You may be wondering, *If I am so important to God, why am I going through such a long drought, such a tough journey? If he really loves me, why am I hitting a brick wall on each interview and seemingly on each path I undertake? Why do I feel like I'm alone in all of this if God is by my side? Why does it seem like every move I make is a mistake? When will it all end?!*

I get that. On one hand, the apostle Paul writes in Romans 8:32 that the Lord will "give us all things." And that seems to cover the need for a job, right? But here's the twist. The Lord knows you and me better than we know ourselves. On the surface we may believe that getting a job is our most pressing need. Yet the Lord may be using this season of transition to weed out the pride, arrogance, self-reliance or other emotional or spiritual deficiencies that a career easily masks. In that respect, he is giving us a true gift — one that will serve us well in the days ahead.

We can truly trust the Lord because he didn't spare his own Son. He assures us that he is in control, he will always provide what is best for us, and he may be using this season of transition for our ultimate good. That's what Romans 8:28 says: "We know that in all things God works for the good of those who love him, who have been called according to his purpose."

If God is working behind the scenes in all things for our good, that insight should set us free to praise him in all things — including when an interview goes poorly, when a job offer doesn't come through or when the funds are getting so low that we have to make another withdrawal from our retirement account. In all things we will trust that God is on our side — for he loved us enough to sacrifice his only Son.

POINTS TO PONDER:

What situations have occurred in your journey that you thought were devastating? Can you see now where the Lord protected you from the wrong decision? What issues have hindered you because of you feeling a need for perfection?

_____

_____

_____

_____

_____

_____

_____

_____

_____

_____

_____

_____

_____

_____

_____

_____

_____

_____

_____

_____

_____

_____

_____

HELP WANTED:

Dear Father, help me realize that since you are for me no one can ultimately be against me. Why do I so easily ignore the One who gave his most precious Son for my eternal life? Help me to see your hand in every job interview and in every lack of response, as well as in every positive affirmation. Help me to trust in your decisions for my life and this journey — for I know that no one loves me more than you. In your holy name I pray. Amen and Amen.

**"You may ask me for anything in my name,
and I will do it."** —JOHN 14:14

Have you ever questioned the Lord regarding this promise from his Word? Is it really true that we can ask for *anything* in Jesus' name, and he will do it?

I'll admit that I've had my doubts, especially during my extended season of unemployment. I remember wondering why, if this promise is true, my pleadings for work remained unanswered. I even started to question if this Scripture was meant to be taken literally. Maybe it was just a way of saying that God will be with us.

Don't get me wrong. I believe the Bible is the inspired and infallible Word of God. But my circumstances created doubt in my heart that such a promise could be true.

The answer came to me the other day while I was revisiting this passage. Once again, my first reaction was to question the Lord. If this is true, how come I'm not working in a better job and making great money, like I was a few years ago? Lord, why does it seem like you're ignoring me? It feels like you're only half-listening when I pray, sort of the way I half-listen to my children when they ask for something.

This time the Lord answered. Not in an audible voice that sounded like Charlton Heston or Morgan Freeman with lots of reverberation. But nonetheless, in my spirit I heard him say, *Keep reading.*

Keep reading?

Keep reading all of what I am saying.

I decided to look at the context of the promise by reading several verses before and after John 14:14. In verse 13, Jesus said, "I will do whatever you ask in my name, so that the Father may be glorified in the Son." In other words, Jesus will give me what I ask for in his name *if* it will glorify the Father. This isn't about you and me getting whatever is on our wish lists. God isn't a celestial vending machine. Rather, our requests should glorify him.

There's more. In verse 15, Jesus went on to say, "If you love me, keep my commands." In today's sales language, that's the "kicker." In other words, you and I can't expect to get what we ask for in prayer unless we are walking in obedience to the Lord and unless the fulfillment of that prayer will glorify God. You see, more than anything, Jesus wants his children to come to him and seek his face. That intimacy is bound to produce a desire to seek God's glory in all our requests.

I am prompted to ask, then, where I am spending most of my time. Praying, studying the Word and praising God? Not me! I'm out there trying to make something happen. I'm trying to show people that I'm the best possible candidate for the position they're trying to fill. I'm trying to figure out how I'm going to pay the rent and what I can do to create income and ultimately wealth.

I am so hung up on what *I* need to do and what *I* can create and what *I* can affect that I don't usually have any time left for the Lord. Oh maybe I get a devotion reading in, or I glance at Scripture on Sunday or Wednesday at church. But every day? Are you kidding? I just don't have the time. However, if I'm not obeying the Lord, am I really asking for things that will glorify him?

Does this sound a bit like your situation and schedule? Are you so busy running around that you're unable to find time to stop and listen for God's plan for your life? Why not try what I'm beginning to do and make time for the Lord? Daily. And when you're right with him you can be confident that you're praying according to his will, and that he will do it — for his glory.

POINTS TO PONDER:

How many days a week do you seek the Lord first? How many situations occur during your journey that the Lord is not first in your thoughts or on your list of priorities? Why not start listing each time you seek him first — beginning with today — and then reflect upon the results as you revisit and review your list.

_____

_____

_____

_____

_____

_____

_____

_____

_____

_____

_____

_____

_____

_____

_____

_____

_____

_____

HELP WANTED:

Dear Lord, I know I need to be willing for you to force me to slow down and make time for you. I know I need to order my priorities so that you are number one on my list every day. Help me to remember that my ultimate goal should always be to glorify you. Give me rest in the knowledge that you will only allow me to reach my journey's end when it is in your perfect plan and will glorify you, not me. In your holy name I pray. Amen and Amen.

**Those who live according to the flesh have their minds set on
what the flesh desires; but those who live in accordance with the Spirit
have their minds set on what the Spirit desires. The mind governed by
the flesh is death, but the mind governed by the Spirit is life and peace.
The mind governed by the flesh is hostile to God; it does not submit
to God's law, nor can it do so. Those who are in the realm
of the flesh cannot please God. —ROMANS 8:5–8**

I have had many jobs and many different life experiences. I have known the life of an executive making more money in one year than many make in ten years, including spending $600 per night for a hotel suite and tipping the wait staff $100. I have also experienced the dread of wondering how I would pay for the next meal, make the next mortgage payment, and scrape enough money together to put gas in the car. I have been a manual laborer, an accountant, a salesman, a sales manager, a president, a CEO, a CFO, a COO — and in a career transition in which I felt like I was a loser and a failure.

Guess what? Through all of this I have been a child of the living God. And there is nothing more important than that reality. The problem is that I often allow my immediate circumstances to define who I am, instead of remembering *whose* I am. Rather than having my mind "set on what the Spirit desires," I've made the mistake of having my mind "governed by the flesh" (Romans 8:5 – 6).

Does this sound familiar? You see, I believe we all know God has a plan for us. We are just so used to being in control of our life situations (or at least we think we are) that we are afraid to let go, since we don't really believe God will be there for us. What's more, we quickly forget that we were "bought at a price" and therefore we belong to him (1 Corinthians 6:19 – 20). I would do well to remember "whose I am" rather than "who I am" as defined by a job.

Christian speaker Bill Karlson talks about LBA — "life by accident." Here's an example: You study to become an accountant, and become an accountant. You begin making more money, get a bigger house, work your way up the corporate ladder, and the cycle continues. Then one day your company decides to replace you with two younger accountants whom they can pay less money than they have been paying you. Thank you, and good-bye. Now what?

Then there's what I call LBN — "life by necessity." This occurs when circumstances require you to take any job that's available in order to make money. Sometimes LBN requires you to abandon your dreams. You may even have a number of different jobs and be forced to learn about a variety of different industries. Sooner or later life by necessity gives way to life by accident as someone with more experience comes along and is willing to work for less money. Thank you, and good-bye. Now what?

Whether you are suffering from LBA or LBN, the result is the same. You are in a career transition and you need to figure out what you want to be when you grow up. I would encourage you to view this as a blessing. You see, through all of these journeys you gained knowledge, wisdom and experience. These are the hidden blessings in all of our stories. The Lord allows you and me to grow and mature and gain experiences that he can use in the future. So stop fretting about who you (someone in transition) are, and take heart knowing *whose* you are — a child of God's.

POINTS TO PONDER:

What do you need to turn over to the Lord? What areas of your journey are you holding on to without seeking the Lord's will? List them, and then experience real freedom and love as he addresses those areas.

_____

_____

_____

_____

_____

_____

_____

_____

_____

_____

_____

_____

_____

_____

_____

_____

_____

HELP WANTED:

Dear heavenly Father, I know you want the very best for me because I am your child. And I know you know what that is. I know, but I struggle to believe. Help me, Lord, to be a believer — a true believer who recognizes your will for my journey and my life. Dear Jesus, not my will but yours be done today and always. I pray for discernment and commit myself to childlike obedience, for your love for me is unconditional and always evident. In your holy name I pray. Amen and Amen.

LESSONS FROM MY GPS

> Trust in the LORD with all your heart and lean not on your own understanding; in all your ways submit to him, and he will make your paths straight. Do not be wise in your own eyes; fear the LORD and shun evil. This will bring health to your body and nourishment to your bones. —PROVERBS 3:5–8

A headline in the April 23, 2012 edition of *The Atlantic* recently grabbed my attention: *53% of Recent College Grads Are Jobless or Underemployed — How?* Think about how alarming that statistic really is — more than half of all college students are graduating only to find there isn't a job in their chosen field waiting for them. After four years of study, many have to set aside their plans to pursue their dreams, settling instead for flipping hamburgers, selling coffee or sweeping floors.

There's nothing wrong with those tasks. In fact, I believe much can be learned by engaging in manual labor. Whether you're reading this as one of those "underemployed" recent college grads or you're a seasoned professional who has been forced to deliver pizza or stock supermarket shelves, I'm here to tell you that the path you're on is part of God's plan for your life. Let me illustrate with a personal example.

When I lost my job as a "big-time" executive, I had to humble myself and take whatever I could find to do just to keep some income coming in. That included freelancing as a locksmith for a very gracious brother from church. My task typically consisted of assisting people who had locked themselves out of their car. One particularly busy day I was on a roll with 14 calls in a 12-hour period. Those calls had me zigzagging from one end of the county to the other to rescue stranded drivers.

I recall thinking about the many times I passed by the same landmarks. I wondered why that person or this person couldn't have locked themselves out just 40 minutes earlier when I was in their area! I began to retrace my routes in my mind and realized what a maze of turns and curves and overlaps had occurred throughout my travels. It was a MapQuest nightmare!

When I read the words in Proverbs 3:6 about how the Lord "will make your paths straight," I was reminded of the haphazard route I had to take while working as a locksmith on that crazy, busy day — which, in turn, prompted me to think about my career path. Specifically, I reflected on how often I have worked at a job in which I had no idea how that role would fit into my future. As I reviewed my experiences in light of this verse, I realized that my assortment of jobs was not a maze of uncharted destinations. In fact, every bit of experience I have accumulated, in many different fields, I am using today. I have to believe that every job you have had has helped to mold you too.

You and I are a MapQuest trip "in process." If you look closely, you can see how the Lord has mapped out your life and how seemingly unrelated job experiences really do fit together to formulate the Lord's plan for you. The experiences of your life and career actually do make sense — you just might not see the big picture at the moment. Unfortunately, that's because you and I are not privy to the directions beyond this very minute.

Although we still want to ask when this part of the journey will be over, and we still long to know where we will end up with our career, we can rest assured that God has a perfect plan for us. He will make your paths straight if you trust in him rather than in yourself. Why not take some time right now and look back over your road map? Isn't it amazing how the Lord has worked, in all things, for your good? If you don't see the straight road just yet, don't worry. With his guidance, you will see how the road behind is part of the road ahead.

POINTS TO PONDER:

As you look in the rear-view mirror, where do you see decisions you made without seeking the Lord's guidance? When were you so lost that you kept hitting dead ends?

Now look back and consider the smooth roads of God's leading in your life. Spend some time praying for the decisions that you face today, asking him to direct your path.

_____

_____

_____

_____

_____

_____

_____

_____

_____

_____

_____

_____

_____

_____

_____

_____

HELP WANTED:

Heavenly Father, help me to see clearly the road map I have traveled. Help me to learn from my past and recognize you in my journey. Most of all I pray you will close doors and place roadblocks when I stray from your perfect path for me in the future. I ask you to help me learn to be more open to your leading and accept correction when I choose my path instead of yours. You know where I will end up — and it will be the perfect place as long as I stay close to you and truly seek your will for my life. In Jesus' name I pray. Amen and Amen.

COMFORT: FOR YOU *AND* TO SHARE

Praise be to the God and Father of our Lord Jesus Christ, the Father of compassion and the God of all comfort, who comforts us in all our troubles, so that we can comfort those in any trouble with the comfort we ourselves receive from God. For just as we share abundantly in the sufferings of Christ, so also our comfort abounds through Christ. —2 CORINTHIANS 1:3–5

Have you ever noticed how a passage from the Bible sort of sneaks up on you sometimes? Whether you're reading the Bible, a devotional book or just reflecting, occasionally a verse will suddenly jump out at you. Sometimes the words of a Scripture will dog me throughout the day — following me around like a lost puppy. I believe that's the Holy Spirit's way of getting a message to me in those moments, even when I'm not fully paying attention.

I've also encountered times when a specific Bible verse is given to me from multiple sources, such as by a friend, in a sermon, or by hearing someone reference it in a conversation. This redundancy occurs in my life when the Lord is really trying to communicate a message to me but I'm not listening.

Not long ago I had one of those weeks. It started when my pastor delivered a sermon in a series he entitled "Wiping of Tears." The cornerstone Bible text was 2 Corinthians 1:3 – 5. Then, after a networking meeting Tuesday night, a local recruiter — a dear friend who was one of the panel members that evening — handed me a sheet of paper with nothing but these same three verses printed on it. And finally, the highlighted passage at our midweek praise and worship service was 2 Corinthians 1:3 – 5.

Clearly the Lord knew that I was in need of comfort — a word that is used five times in this brief passage. I'm not surprised by his proactive effort to help me hear his voice. After all, he knows the issues and challenges I face, just as he is fully aware of your circumstances. In addition to juggling a myriad of tasks related to my job transition, I was spending a lot of time helping my sister who had sustained a head injury in a car accident, leaving her incapable of working due to limited cognitive-processing abilities. Naturally I stepped in to help her navigate a mountain of paper shuffling required by workers' comp, the doctors, the post office where she was employed and the claims manager.

Though glad to help, I was overwhelmed to the point of despair. My patience with my sister's situation and her quest for answers from multiple bureaucracies had pushed me to the brink. I wanted to be out from under the pressure of getting it all done, on top of needing to prepare for various job interviews and networking opportunities and dealing with the emotional roller coaster of rejection that was becoming a way of life. I remember thinking, *Why does it have to be me that helps her, anyway?*

That's when 2 Corinthians 1:3 – 5 was brought to my attention through that sermon ... and again by a friend ... and for the third time in the praise and worship service. I realized that while God certainly comforts us in all our troubles for our own benefit, there's another important reason for his gift of comfort: "so that we can comfort those in any trouble with the comfort we ourselves receive from God." In other words, the Lord provides comfort in our situations and, in turn, commissions us to comfort others just as he comforts us. Wow, what a wake-up call!

Do you need comfort today in your job transition? In your personal life? In your relationships? In dealing with the rejection of not getting that interview? Whatever the situation may be, what you're facing is never bigger than the Lord's outflow of comfort. Seek the comfort he has for you, and rest in it. Then reach out to others in need. Let his comfort pass through you to those who need his comfort too.

POINTS TO PONDER:

Read Psalm 73:26, Luke 4:18 and 2 Corinthians 4:8 – 10,16 – 18. What do these Scriptures teach us about comfort during times of affliction? Can you think of a situation in which someone in your life was brought to you for some much-needed comfort? Do you know someone who is struggling to find work and would surely appreciate your effort to reach out and show that you care?

_____

_____

_____

_____

_____

_____

_____

_____

_____

_____

_____

_____

_____

_____

_____

_____

_____

HELP WANTED:

Dear Lord Jesus, I pray you will grant me ears that truly hear and a spirit that truly listens. Rather than always thinking about my own needs, enable me to be more aware of those you bring to me in need of comfort. Lord, help me to be selfless rather than selfish. You never let me down; you always provide for my needs. Thank you, Father! In your holy name I pray. Amen and Amen.

"Lord, if it's you," Peter replied, "tell me to come to you on the water." "Come," he said. Then Peter got down out of the boat, walked on the water and came toward Jesus. But when he saw the wind, he was afraid and, beginning to sink, cried out, "Lord, save me!" Immediately Jesus reached out his hand and caught him. "You of little faith," he said, "why did you doubt?" —MATTHEW 14:28–31

When you woke up this morning, what was the forecast? I'm not talking about the weather conditions; I'm referring to your outlook for the day. Was it bright and sunny — reflecting, perhaps, your positive attitude about your prospects of finding work? Or is your outlook dim? Is a sea of doubt washing over your self-confidence? Have you been rocked by a storm of rejection at the hands of one employer after another? Are mounting bills ready to capsize what little resolve you have to press on?

If that's you, today's passage offers great promise. All you and I have to do is cast our troubles on Jesus and stay focused on him. If we keep our eyes fixed on him, we'll be able to walk through anything we encounter — even life's strongest winds and waves. This is so powerful yet so simple, if we just trust the call of Jesus when he beckons us. And yet I know I spent most of my time during my transition spitting out saltwater because I doubted. In fact, my full-time job often seemed to be treading water.

If you're like me, you spend quite a bit of time wondering whether what you hear when you pray is from the Holy Spirit or the great deceiver. Even when we believe the Lord is speaking to us, we often question his leading for a long time before we yield. And like Peter in this story, if we step out in faith and follow his call, our circumstances tempt us to question the decision to follow him.

For instance, has the Lord opened a door for a job that feels beneath you? Or has he led you to serve in a church or nonprofit organization, but you resist because there's no money in it? That was me. I clearly heard the Lord tell me he wanted me to serve him by ministering to those in a career crisis. My response was, but Lord, what if there's no money? What if people don't come to my seminars? What if I screw things up and don't help people, but instead my advice makes things worse? What if? What if? What if?

My response should have been, *OK, Lord, if you are for me, who could possibly be against me?* Instead, I rehearsed a litany of concerns about *my* well-being, *my* security, and *my* desires and preferences. This demonstrated nothing less than a lack of trust in my heavenly Father, who knows what is best for me — and for you.

I'm not trying to sugarcoat reality. I'm a real person, living in the real world: a world that requires me to pay the rent and the car payment; buy gas, clothing and food; care for my children; and on and on and on. And do you know what?

God knows all about it!

In fact, he knew about it before I was even born. He knew what my life would be like and he knew the plan he had for me. All I have to do is trust him and follow him in the midst of my personal storm. I need to stop worrying about me and start looking at him. What he has for me is far better than anything I could even dream of. So why am I not obeying?

Are you ready to turn it over to Jesus — I mean *really* turn it over to Jesus? If so, then step out of the boat and focus only on him. Follow him and don't look back. Stop the whining, the complaining, the "Woe is me" and the "What-ifs." Make today your first day of the new journey with him at the controls.

POINTS TO PONDER:

What fears plague you and prevent you from moving forward? List the situations in your journey that have kept you from stepping out on the water. What do you think might happen if you were to let go and let God lead you, even when the waves of life are crashing around you?

_____

_____

_____

_____

_____

_____

_____

_____

_____

_____

_____

_____

_____

_____

_____

_____

_____

HELP WANTED:

Heavenly Father, I often feel like the boat is filling with water and I'm about to drown — like I can barely tread water until help comes from I don't know where. I pray for true belief, for trust in you that surpasses any and every trial in my life. I pray I will really seek you and fix my gaze on you and not on myself and what I can do. Hold me tight, dear Father. Comfort me, and help me to feel the security of your agape love. In your holy name I pray. Amen and Amen.

TAKE A REST

"Come to me, all you who are weary and burdened, and I will give you rest."
— MATTHEW 11:28

There's a story of two friends who liked to engage in "manly man" challenges —
such as determining who could catch the biggest fish or climb a mountain faster.
One Saturday these guys decided to try their hand at sawing timber. Armed with
two chainsaws and a can of gas, early that morning they headed to a wooded
piece of property one of them owned. The owner of the property, we'll call him
Luke, challenged his friend "Jimmy" to a contest. Whoever could cut up the larg-
est pile of fallen timber in six hours would be the winner.

For the first couple of hours they both worked nonstop. With the sun bear-
ing down on them, they worked up a serious sweat. As the afternoon progressed,
their arms, legs and lower back started to hurt. For his part, Luke didn't stop.
When he looked across the field, though, he noticed Jimmy was sitting down —
again. An hour later, Luke smiled when he saw Jimmy sitting down for a third
time, figuring he would definitely be the winner since he had yet to take a break.

When they took inventory of their work at the end of the day, Luke was
stunned to see that Jimmy had a much larger stack of wood. When Luke asked
how that was possible, Jimmy answered, "Sure, when I sat down I took a little
break — but I was also sharpening my saw!"

There's a lesson in this story if you are fighting the usual battles of life plus
going through a career transition. Listen to me. There is no shame in being weary
and needing to rest. *It is OK to take a rest.* Indeed, we would do well to build in
time to "sharpen our saws."

Have you been waiting for someone to tell you it's OK to take a break? I often
felt that way when I was without full-time work. If I wasn't employed, how could
I possibly be worn out? The fact of the matter was that I had been spending about
as many hours a day trying to find a new opportunity as I did working when I was
employed in my last position! Although I didn't give up when I was without work,
I sure grew weary of those immovable walls. I found that I had to walk away from
things until I was stronger and ready to take another run at landing work.

If we're honest, we all get tired and weary; we lose our temper and even our faith at times. This *does not* make you a bad person or an unfaithful loser. The fact that we need rest just demonstrates that we are human. Jesus recognized this and knew we would go through times long on problems and short on solutions. "Come to me, all you who are weary and burdened, and I will give you rest" (Matthew 11:28). The Lord never tells us to give up — quite the opposite. He says rest is available for us when we are weary.

Look at it this way. In order to be weary, we must be fighting the fight, right? So if you are in the grips of a career transition, or working in a place where you get no respect, or working some job just to pay the bills for the time being, you are in the battle. And that's not the only battle you are fighting. How about family dynamics that can reach the breaking point under the stress of no income? Or the need to figure out how to maintain your vehicle's reliability so you can get to an interview? You face a long list of battlefronts, which is why downtime is so important.

Just remember, we're talking about taking a rest from the battle — not a rest from life. Use your break to "sharpen your saw," but then get right back in the battle for that next opportunity. In the words of Sir Winston Churchill, "Never give in. Never give in. Never, never, never, never — in nothing, great or small, large or petty — never give in, except to convictions of honor and good sense."

POINTS TO PONDER:

Make a list of everything that is burdening and weighing you down today. Then go down the list and release yourself from each burden. Feel the rest. Every time you begin to feel worn out, review the list and release each one to the Lord anew, asking him to give you the freedom to rest.

_____

_____

_____

_____

_____

_____

_____

_____

_____

_____

_____

_____

_____

_____

_____

_____

_____

HELP WANTED:

Dear Lord Jesus, I admit I need rest. I need you to give me emotional permission to stop and unwind. I ask you, Father, to take away the feeling of guilt, because I just can't go any further. Give me rest; grant me the spiritual and emotional OK to take time to recharge. Help me to come to you, trust in you, and gain the rest only you are able to provide. In your holy name I pray. Amen and Amen.

> "Truly I tell you, if you have faith as small as a mustard seed,
> you can say to this mountain, 'Move from here to there,' and it will move.
> Nothing will be impossible for you." —MATTHEW 17:20

On Tuesday mornings I meet with a number of guys in a group called the Samson Society. Founded by Nate Larkin, the Samson Society is an informal network where men connect with other men in the spirit of accountability. Our conversations are honest, real and confidential, in a no-holds-barred environment. The premise is to find a "Silas" — someone who will walk with you through life and contact you every day. Your Silas is your go-to guy. No matter what is happening in your life, your Silas is the guy to call. This is probably the most eye-opening, weight-lifting, personal growth activity I have ever participated in.

Recently the topic was faith. I really didn't want to deal with faith, as the week wasn't shaping up to be all that great and there were some financial issues I had been worrying about. My faith quotient was running a bit low. One of the men excused himself from the group, returning a few minutes later with a jar of mustard seeds.

Now I was very familiar with Matthew 17:20. I have conducted numerous coaching meetings with people in transition and have told them to embrace faith as small as a mustard seed. At the same time, I admit I had never seen a mustard seed before — although I figured it must be small or Jesus wouldn't have used that analogy. My friend took a mustard seed out of the bottle and passed the bottle around, telling the guys to take just one seed.

The first person took a seed and passed the bottle. Guess what? He was immediately rebuked because he took not one but *two* mustard seeds. When the bottle came to me, I couldn't believe how tiny they were. Taking one seed from the bottle, I was immediately hit with the object lesson. Interestingly, I was the fourth person around the circle to get the bottle, and by the time I received it the first guy had already lost his mustard seed. It was so small, you didn't even realize it was in your hand. It has no weight at all.

Is it really possible that my faith is less than the size of one mustard seed? How about your faith? Allow me to encourage you to go to the kitchen or the store and get a bottle of mustard seeds. Look at the size of one seed and remember the Lord said that if you have faith as small as a mustard seed, "nothing will be impossible for you." That's a promise straight from the heart of Jesus.

That encounter with a mustard seed sure made me think long and hard about how much time I spend worrying about Number One — me — and how little time I spend with the Lord. I'm talking about quality time when I'm not distracted by the TV, radio, books, conversations or wandering thoughts, or worrying about something while I'm praying. Memorizing Scripture, singing hymns and songs of praise, and attending church are really important elements of the Christian life. Nothing, however, is a replacement for quality time spent alone with Jesus. I know I don't spend enough time in prayer and conversation with the Lord. How about you?

Why not commit to getting a jar of your own mustard seeds? Place the jar in a prominent place where you'll see it often. Consider placing a few seeds in small containers in your car, by your computer, and in other spots in your house. Then remember that having faith the size of one little mustard seed is our goal — faith that the Lord will provide all you need today and throughout your career transition. Sound a bit crazy? Well, maybe — but what have you got to lose?

A mustard seed ... Is that so much to risk?

POINTS TO PONDER:

"If you have faith as small as a mustard seed" ... What in your life requires faith? How many times in just the past few days has your faith fallen short of mustard-seed size? Commit to getting a mustard seed this week and keeping it in a frequented location — maybe in a baggie so you don't lose it. During the week, jot down the times when this reminder impacts your ability to turn things over to the Lord.

_____

_____

_____

_____

_____

_____

_____

_____

_____

_____

_____

_____

_____

_____

_____

_____

HELP WANTED:

Lord Jesus, I am rebuked in my spirit every time I read this verse. All you ask is for me to have faith the size of a mustard seed, and I don't make the grade. Help me, Father, to keep you first in my life in all things. I rededicate my life to you, and I pray that a little mustard seed will pale in comparison to my new commitment to you. In Jesus' name I pray. Amen and Amen.

"However, I consider my life worth nothing to me; my only aim is to finish the race and complete the task the Lord Jesus has given me — the task of testifying to the good news of God's grace." —ACTS 20:24

Here are three of the most difficult questions we wrestle with during our career transition journey: (1) What does God want from me? (2) Where does God want me to serve? (3) What life lesson does God want me to learn in this trial? As we seek answers to those questions, an underlying restlessness sometimes bubbles to the surface in a flash of genuine, unvarnished honesty.

In that unguarded, unbridled moment we give voice to our deepest emotions, saying, *God, I have had enough. It's time for you to show me my next job. I have waited a long time, and I am running low on money and even lower on self-worth and patience. I am yelling at my spouse, children, friends and everyone else brave enough to enter the perimeter of my attention. I am waiting, God. Why is it taking you so long to show up?*

This may be a bit stronger than the way you're handling your transition. Maybe you have a different way of venting your deepest feelings, but the meaning of the plea is the same. If you're like me, you want some *action*. When I worked in business, I was results-driven. I had to produce, and I had deadlines — multiple deadlines — daily. I worked in an environment where there were expectations to live up to. I'm sure you know the drill. And now, after years of facing and meeting deadlines, you're waiting for God to act. This is unfamiliar territory: a place where you have no control, no deadlines, no action plan, not even a projection from God regarding his timeline.

He is in complete and total control of your journey, and I bet you don't like it! Me neither.

OK, there you have it. I don't like the fact that I'm not in control of this situation. Furthermore, what if this is it? What if the Lord wants you and me to serve exactly where we are today? What if your future is *not* going to be serving him in business as a highly paid executive? What if you'll *never* land that cherished job as a teacher or professor? What if he wants you to serve him by serving others?

What if poverty is in your future? What if you're exactly where he wants you to be? Come to think of it, that may be the scariest thought of all.

I share those feelings. I have been telling others how the Lord will place me where he wants me to be. But all the time I'm thinking, in the back of my mind, that surely he wants me back in the business world running a company, with all of the benefits. This ministry stuff sure helps a ton of folks, but it isn't really "it." Nonprofit work can't be where he wants me long-term, can it?

So far the answer is yes. This *is* where he wants me to serve. That means he will supply my needs — certainly not my wants, but my needs. What about you? Where are you today? What if this is exactly where the Lord wants you to be for a long time? Will you answer the call? Will you serve where he plants you? Or will you fight his will in order to acquire that higher-paying job you want? What if the Lord is using you to touch people's lives right where you are?

If you accept where God has placed you today with faith, hope and joy, congratulations — he will use you and give you peace and contentment like you have never known. That doesn't mean it will be easy. You might have to learn to live on less. But God will be promoting his kingdom through you. What could be a better place than the center of his will?

POINTS TO PONDER:

Where are you right now? Not just in transition — where are you in your life? If you could write your own ticket, where would it take you? Where might the Lord be calling you to serve? What's keeping you from pursuing that leading?

_____

_____

_____

_____

_____

_____

_____

_____

_____

_____

_____

_____

_____

_____

_____

_____

_____

_____

_____

_____

_____

HELP WANTED:

Heavenly Father, I pray you will calm my spirit and my heart at this time. Help me look to you for my needs. Help me to accept whatever you provide. Help me to serve in a way that I might not have even considered before. Open my heart to your calling, whatever it may be. In you alone I will seek my peace, and I will be content. In your holy name I pray. Amen and Amen.

HE WILL PROVIDE

LORD, you are the God who saves me; day and night I cry out to you.
May my prayer come before you; turn your ear to my cry. —PSALM 88:1–2

Do you experience times when you are wearied with the "what" questions. You know … What is my calling? What career would really make me happy? What am I genuinely passionate about doing? What if I take a job that I don't like? What if I bomb the interview — again? Because these kinds of questions cut so deep, after a while it hurts to think about them. In fact, when the "what" questions start to swirl around in your head, I imagine you'd like to forget about your career transition journey and concentrate on something else — maybe look up random stuff on eBay, surf the Internet, go to lunch, work in the yard or just take a nap — *anything* to escape for a couple of hours.

I get that. There were times during my transition that were so bleak, so dark, so discouraging, that I felt like I was plunging into a downward spiral of depression. These words from Psalm 88 described my emotional state well: "I am overwhelmed with troubles and my life draws near to death. I am counted among those who go down to the pit; I am like one without strength" (verses 3–4). Ironically, I took comfort from this psalm, knowing that I wasn't alone in feeling that "darkness is my closest friend" (verse 18).

Thankfully, I am blessed to relate to a number of Christian brothers every week. When those feelings of despair started to drag me down, I knew I could talk to one of those friends. And I did. These men held me accountable, helped me work on my game plan for the journey and enabled me to stay "real" in my expectations. Most important, they loved me through the tough days, which prevented me from spiraling too deep.

There are times when you need more than comfort from a trusted friend. You would benefit from seeing a Christian counselor or speaking with your pastor. Hear me — there is no shame in seeking a professional adviser. Proverbs 15:22 says, "Plans fail for lack of counsel, but with many advisers they succeed." The point is, don't try to make this journey alone.

In addition to the need for close friends and advisers during the journey, I have found it beneficial, when I'm really struggling with those pesky "what" questions, to shift the focus to a different "what" — namely, *what I have*. There's something about giving thanks for my blessings that chases away the doldrums of despair. Here's a short list of blessings I have compiled:

1. **RELATIONSHIPS:** I'm blessed with a loving family, faithful friends and great neighbors.

2. **HEALTH:** I walk, talk, see and hear; I have use of my fingers, hands, arms, feet and legs; and I'm not physically or mentally disabled.

3. **PROVISION:** I have a place to live, electricity, heat and air conditioning, food, a reliable car, gas in the car, clothing, a phone, a cell phone, a computer.

4. **A CARING CHURCH:** Pastors, elders, deacons and counselors are available to help provide for my spiritual, emotional and even financial needs (through the deacon fund).

5. **A GOD WHO LOVES ME:** The Lord knew I would be on this journey. He has not abandoned me. He is my Provider and "the God who saves me" (Psalm 88:1).

The list can go on and on. Sometimes I need it to go on and on for me to really get the message that God does care. In his time, he will supply the answers to the "what" questions. Our job is to have faith and believe.

POINTS TO PONDER:

List the people you can genuinely trust with everything you are dealing with in your life. This may be a very short list; in fact, it's OK if there's only one name on it.

_____

_____

_____

_____

_____

_____

_____

_____

_____

_____

_____

_____

_____

_____

_____

_____

Now list the things you really need to unload. Take this list to your trust-worthy friend and talk through each concern. Read and reflect on Lamentations 3:22 – 23.

_____

_____

_____

_____

_____
_____
_____
_____
_____
_____
_____
_____
_____
_____
_____
_____
_____

HELP WANTED:

I am so blessed by you, Lord. Tears come to my eyes when I take time to consider all you have given me. You have assured me that I would never walk alone, and you have kept that promise. Thank you for being my Friend, my Father and my "go-to God" whenever I need to unload. Thank you for bringing into my life people with whom I can be truly honest. My cup overflows. In your holy name I pray. Amen and Amen.

FOR YOUR OWN GOOD

We know that in all things God works for the good of those who love him, who have been called according to his purpose. —ROMANS 8:28

When I was ten years old my father died. I believe this is the reason I have some difficulty understanding and accepting the relationship I have with my heavenly Father. I understand the concept of having to experience situations in order to learn. I know some of the best lessons I have experienced in life have been the result of making it through a tough situation. I know what love is — but I'm not sure I really grasp *unconditional* love.

When I became a father I experienced unconditional love, from the giving perspective of a parent. However, I don't think I fully understand unconditional love from the receiving perspective. I know that for the Lord to give his only Son to endure shame, brutality and a horrible death for my sake means that his love is immeasurable. But *immeasurable* and *unconditional* are two very different things. What does unconditional love look like?

I've heard unconditional love described this way: No matter what I do, no matter what I say, God still loves me. I can make a mess of my life, I can miss church on Sunday, I can get depressed and eat too much, I can mismanage my funds and be a poor steward of my resources, I can even be mean to my family — yet God still loves me!

Okay, I can accept that in my head. But what about in real-world situations? How about when I get a phone call with the bad news that I didn't get the job, or when there's no response to the dozens of résumés I've mailed out, or when an interview goes bad and I feel like I blew it in spite of my preparation? Does God still love me?

I confess that it's tough, in those circumstances, to accept that I am experiencing the unconditional love of God. Why? Because I reason that if God loved me, I'd have a job. If God loved me unconditionally, I wouldn't be afraid to go to the mailbox to retrieve the stack of unpaid bills or the notices from the IRS, because in my mind he would have provided the work I seek. Much of the time, candidly, during my transition journey, I didn't feel loved — and certainly not loved unconditionally.

This begs the question: How can we relate to our heavenly Father and know that he loves us with an unconditional love when bad things happen? Consider these words from Romans 8:28: "In all things God works for the good of those who love him." You see, God allows trials and difficult circumstances to happen for our good, for our benefit. Trials come so we can learn from them, because he is preparing you and me for what he has ahead for us in life. "The Lord disciplines the one he loves, and he chastens everyone he accepts as his son" (Hebrews 12:6).

Do you believe the Lord loves you unconditionally? Do you believe he is doing what is best for you? Do you believe that by the end of your transition journey you are going to be stronger and better able to face the future? Are you ready to push ahead on this journey knowing that God is working for your good?

Indeed, my prayer is that God will reveal to you the best possible direction for your life. But more important, I pray that you experience his unconditional love today and every day.

POINTS TO PONDER:

The Scriptures are clear that the Lord loves us unconditionally. Are you experiencing his unconditional love in your life? List the times during this journey in which you have questioned if he is working for your good. Pray over your list and ask God to show you how he is working for your good in each situation.

_____

_____

_____

_____

_____

_____
_____
_____
_____
_____
_____
_____
_____
_____
_____
_____
_____
_____
_____

HELP WANTED:

Dear heavenly Father, I am often weary from your tests in my life. I often feel discouraged and unworthy. And yes, I often feel this unconditional love concept is beyond my understanding. But Lord Jesus, you are "the way and the truth and the life" (John 14:6) and "the light of the world" (John 8:12) — the light for everything that happens in my journey. I pray for perseverance and steadfastness as I complete this test of my faith and hope in you. In your magnificent name I pray. Amen and Amen.

> The Lord will guide you always; he will satisfy your needs
> in a sun-scorched land and will strengthen your frame.
> You will be like a well-watered garden, like a spring whose
> waters never fail. —ISAIAH 58:11

People who are new to the career transition journey often ask me what they will need the most as they look for work. They're often surprised when I reply that their greatest need will be for strength, and ideally they will receive that strength from a variety of sources. As you probably know from experience, being without a job — especially for an extended period of time — has a way of knocking your legs out from under you. Being fired, released, downsized or squeezed out of a position you once held has a way of weakening your spirit. But to remain in a transition for weeks, months and years zaps your strength until you simply want to give up the pursuit of work — as literally millions have done today.

As we see in Isaiah 58:11, the Lord can "satisfy your needs in a sun-scorched land" and "strengthen your frame." How? I believe the answer lies in tapping into the strength of the Lord as well as a variety of other sources — especially friends and family members upon whose shoulders you can lean. Look at it this way. When God said, "It is not good for the man to be alone. I will make a helper suitable for him" (Genesis 2:18), he was referring to the creation of Eve. I believe God's observation that it was "not good" for the man to be alone, however, extends to the larger dynamic of our need for community, fellowship, companionship and accountability.

Of course, the Lord is "our refuge and strength, an ever-present help in trouble" (Psalm 46:1). But just as God brought Eve to Adam, we would do well to have relationships with people from whom we are able to gain strength and encouragement. This speaks to the need for us to communicate with our families and those closest to us. Why, then, do we try to hide our feelings and our fears from others? How can we have the strength to face rejection after rejection when applying for work if we don't have someone who has our back? Why are we so unwilling to be honest about our concerns with the ones with whom we are supposed to be the closest?

In my case, I was afraid I would be thought of as a loser. If I were to be honest about my feelings, my fears and my anxiety, I was afraid I would lose the esteem of others, as well as my self-respect, authority and control. Most of all, I was afraid I would be accused of not trusting the Lord. Looking back, I realize how my tendency to cocoon kicked in. I stuffed away my frustrations with my job search and refused to let people know my true feelings. Have you ever taken that approach?

Not surprising, since we were designed for fellowship, my relief came from a men's group. You and I need each other to share the load. The apostle Paul wrote, "Carry each other's burdens, and in this way you will fulfill the law of Christ" (Galatians 6:2). These men gave me the opportunity to open up and honestly discuss my grieving process — which, I should add, accompanies every transition journey — and the strength to share things I couldn't share with others. Eventually they helped me realize that I could, in fact, admit to my family my fears, my needs, my discontent with God, my feeling of abandonment and even my lack of faith at times.

I began having a daily accountability phone call with two trusted Christian brothers, which has made all the difference in my life. As a result, I received the strength I needed to get back on track and once again trust in the Lord while standing firm against the lies of the devil. Don't be afraid to talk with your family and with the Lord. If you are open and honest, you will be amazed at how great the feeling of relief can be when that burden is lifted. Why not give it a try today? Talk with your family; talk with the Lord. Together that will "strengthen your frame."

POINTS TO PONDER:

List the people who have helped strengthen you during this journey, and then note what they said or did that gave you strength to carry on. Give God thanks for this, and keep strong by reflecting on this rather than listening to the negativity spoken to you by the devil.

_____

_____

_____

_____

_____

_____

_____

_____

_____

_____

_____

_____

_____

_____

_____

_____

_____

_____

HELP WANTED:

*Dear Father in heaven, you alone provide the true friendship I desire. I know you
have placed people in my life to help me. Give me the humility to seek them out and
to develop a true trust in them. Help me to gain the strength I need from them and
from you. Help me to desire communion with you, dear Father, every day. In your
compassionate name I pray. Amen and Amen.*

When he heard this, Jesus said, "This sickness will not end in death. No, it is for God's glory so that God's Son may be glorified through it." Now Jesus loved Martha and her sister and Lazarus. So when he heard that Lazarus was sick, he stayed where he was two more days, and then he said to his disciples, "Let us go back to Judea." —JOHN 11:4–7

Have you ever wondered why Jesus, when he heard that his dear friend Lazarus was seriously ill, waited two days before going to be with him? Though Jesus' delay seemed inexplicable — at least from the point of view of Lazarus's sisters, who requested his presence — he would be "glorified" because of it. Jesus didn't immediately respond to their request, and the end result revealed that he was indeed the Messiah, the Son of God.

In other words, "silence" was the answer he gave. Yes, the *answer*. That silence turned into an amazing demonstration of deliverance from a situation that Mary, Martha and their neighbors had never known was possible — the resurrection of a person who had died.

Here's the connection to those of us on a transition journey. When we're out of work we continuously ask God to answer our prayer for a new career opportunity. Like King David of Biblical times, we cry out, "Have mercy on me, LORD, for I am faint ... My soul is in deep anguish. How long, LORD, how long?" (Psalm 6:2 – 3). We wonder how long it will be before we get a job — primarily because we assume that a new job is the only possible answer to our prayer.

What's more, we believe anything short of getting a job means that the Lord is ignoring our prayer. We are tempted to believe that he has forsaken us if our prayer isn't answered with a new job. *Doesn't God realize that I am afraid? That I need money? That I need self-esteem? That I need to rebuild my sense of self-worth?*

Actually, God realizes much more than that. He is well aware of our needs, yet his desire is for us to grow closer to him, to trust in him, to experience the marvelous feeling of contentment that comes from a closer walk with him. The fact that Jesus didn't drop everything and rush to Mary and Martha's aid demonstrates that God doesn't operate on our schedule. Clearly we are to operate on *his* schedule. That new job will come through on the exact day and at the exact moment he has planned it for us — and not one minute of worrying will change this.

We can make any bargains we wish with God, we can promise to be all he would want us to be — *when we get that new job*. But the Lord knows us better than we know ourselves. He knows that once we get that new job, we will revert to work-schedule mode and he will take the backseat again — that is, until we need him again.

Granted, we might be afraid; we might be unsure of ourselves and our abilities. We might feel rejected, overlooked and embarrassed, having heard nothing but silence from the Lord in answer to our prayers. If that's you, I encourage you to take this time to know that he is God (see Psalm 46:10; 100:3). Silence is sometimes his answer. Why? Because he wants us to spend more time working on our relationship with him.

Why not take a moment right now to actually praise the Lord for his silence? Praise him for the opportunity to grow closer to him. Enjoy the pleasure of his close company while you have the time to develop that habit of intimacy. Bask in the glory of his silence. Just lean back and feel his presence. It is peace.

POINTS TO PONDER:

Do you truly believe the Lord has paid the price for you? Do you believe he orchestrates all things for your good? Make a list of the times you have not felt this way, the times you felt alone and believed he didn't care because he didn't respond in your time frame. Think back over your career transition journey and examine if he was there, even though he didn't provide the answer you wanted.

_____

_____

_____

_____

_____

_____

_____

_____

_____

_____

_____

_____

_____

_____

_____

_____

_____

_____

_____

_____

HELP WANTED:

Heavenly Father, I know the war has been won! I know you have paid the price for my salvation. I experience great relief every time I think of how you paid for my sins. Emblazon this truth in my heart, Father, so that I will feel this gift from you more often. I should be rejoicing every minute of the day, but instead I have fear and uncertainty. Help me to see you in all I do and in all that happens during this journey. Help me to accept silence as an answer. In your glorious name I pray. Amen and Amen.

FLASHBACKS REVISITED

There is no fear in love. But perfect love drives out fear,
because fear has to do with punishment.
The one who fears is not made perfect in love.— 1 JOHN 4:18

I have a number of friends who served in Vietnam. One thing that seems to be a common thread for all of them is their inability to rid themselves of flashbacks — a sudden recall of the past that feels so real it's as if they were transported back to the scene. Some flashbacks are of war atrocities, others are a living terror beyond my comprehension, while still others are sweet memories of people who were freed or rescued.

One veteran's positive flashback particularly stands out in my mind — that of a young Vietnamese girl who was so happy to see a friendly American soldier that she picked a weed from the grass and, with tears in her eyes, presented it to him. Can you imagine the relief that little child must have felt? And the feeling of accomplishment and hope the soldier felt?

The fact of the matter is that many of us in a career transition suffer from our own set of paralyzing flashbacks. Although they aren't war-related, they are just as real and debilitating. Most of the time they sneak up on us in the form of fear, rejection or inadequacy.

I confess this is an area I still struggle with. I often suffer from flashbacks of the fear and anxiety associated with the day I was terminated. I am also mentally transported back to situations in which I had to admit that I had no job, or to instances in which I had to say no to things my children had always expected and enjoyed. The result is always the same — the pain is revisited. It hurt inside when I experienced my first flashback, and it continues to hurt every time one hits.

While reading 1 John 4:18, it occurred to me that the deeper, underlying problem I wrestle with is fear. Fear of revisiting the past. Fear of having to relive all of the tough times. I know in my head that the Lord has closed the door to the past. So why am I still dwelling on it? The answer is that I haven't embraced the promise that "perfect love drives out fear" — in my *heart*. It's like I'm living my life waiting for the other shoe to drop.

Now when I experience a fear-producing flashback, I remind myself that "fear has to do with punishment" and that "there is no fear in love." Furthermore, I focus on the fact that I have been and am well loved by Jesus, and I know the Lord would not rub my face in my fears. That leaves only one option as to the source of these flashbacks: The devil would just love for me to dwell on the sorrows of the past and to take my mind off of the love and grace I have in Christ. This is why Peter, who knew something about fear and regret (remember how he denied Jesus), warns, "Be alert and of sober mind. Your enemy the devil prowls around like a roaring lion looking for someone to devour" (1 Peter 5:8).

Are you wresting with flashbacks that wound so deeply that you find yourself unable to face the day? Are flashbacks of your termination neutralizing your will and your confidence to approach another potential employer? If so, it's time to call upon the Lord once again, because he alone gives you and me the strength to resist the devil. Then praise the Lord that his perfect love drives out all of our fears.

POINTS TO PONDER:

What flashbacks have found a home in your mind? What impact do these memories of past failures, loss, disappointment or fear have on your efforts to find work? Do you recognize the source of these flashbacks? Spend some time laying each painful memory at the feet of Jesus, and then embrace with your heart the good news that his perfect love drives out all fear!

_____

_____

_____

_____

_____

_____

_____

_____

_____

_____

_____

_____

_____

_____

_____

_____

_____

_____

_____

_____

HELP WANTED:

Heavenly Father, I admit that I often forget you have the paid the price for all of my sins. And I realize that the devil has a strong desire to occupy my every thought and move me farther away from you. I pray you will continue to fill my mind, heart and spirit with the ways you alone have helped me in troubled times. I pray for a closeness to you that I can develop only through your Word and prayer. In Jesus' mighty name I pray. Amen and Amen.

"Be strong and very courageous. Be careful to obey all the law my servant Moses gave you; do not turn from it to the right or to the left, that you may be successful wherever you go. Keep this Book of the Law always on your lips; meditate on it day and night, so that you may be careful to do everything written in it. Then you will be prosperous and successful. Have I not commanded you? Be strong and courageous. Do not be afraid; do not be discouraged, for the LORD your God will be with you wherever you go."
—JOSHUA 1:7–9

If you have ever lost a loved one, you know that certain dates become emblazoned in your memory: the day they passed away, their birthday, perhaps a special occasion you shared together and certainly the holidays. These are the times when we feel the greatest loss of their presence.

Today my older brother, Steven, would have turned 58 years old. We were very close. He and I shared many great moments over the years, and admittedly we shared some fights, disagreements and tough times, as all brothers do. When he died of leukemia and cancer, he was 55 years "young" — a podiatrist, husband, father, uncle, friend and confidant to many.

It makes no sense to me that a man in his prime would be taken from this world. But that was the Lord's plan. If we believe in the risen Messiah, we know that the eternal reward waiting for us is in heaven is so much greater than the life we live here. That is a consolation, but it doesn't replace the pain of loss — the feeling that we have been cheated by not having more time with our departed loved one.

When I was going through an extended period of unemployment, I found myself comparing the way I was handling my transition journey to the way I handled the loss of loved ones. I'm not suggesting the loss of my brother was equivalent to the loss of my career. I'm saying that I recognize a loss is a loss. The emotional reactions to the death of a career are similar to the emotional reactions to losing someone we love. Likewise, a number of similar questions are raised in both scenarios. The tough question that surfaced with my brother's passing is essentially the same core question I often pose to the Lord with reference to my transition: Why did I lose my job at the height of my career?

As I spent time meditating on the Scriptures, the Lord revealed several answers. First of all, if I had remained in the job I had at the time, I surely would have suffered. I was an emotional wreck just waiting for the hammer to fall. In fact, getting out of that work environment was the best thing for me. Looking back over the season that followed my work-related loss, I can now see how I have been able to grow spiritually during my journey. I see that who I am today as a person is much better than who I was as an executive running on fumes.

Where are you today with your loss? Are you still grieving? Or are you ready to accept the Lord's master plan for your life and your future? Are you ready to move forward, knowing that he truly wants what is best for you? Or are you still claiming it wasn't right, it wasn't fair, it shouldn't have been you who lost their employment? Are you ready to accept the love of those around you? Are you taking advantage of the brothers and sisters God has placed in your path to pray for you, assist you, love you and comfort you?

Why not take a moment right now and turn it over to the Lord? It's not a matter of what's right or fair. It's a matter of acceptance — trusting and obeying the only One who can truly comfort you. He who holds your life in his hands invites you to meditate on his Word "day and night" and to be "strong and courageous." As the Lord charged Joshua in preparation of leading the Israelites into the promised land, "Do not be afraid; do not be discouraged, for the LORD your God will be with you wherever you go" (Joshua 1:8 – 9).

POINTS TO PONDER:

As the book of Joshua opens, Joshua is processing both the death of Moses — his leader, mentor and friend — and his marching orders to take on new frontiers. How are you handling the loss of your job? In what ways might that loss cripple you from pursuing new horizons?

_____

_____

_____
_____
_____
_____
_____
_____
_____
_____
_____
_____
_____
_____
_____
_____
_____
_____

HELP WANTED:

Heavenly Father, you have placed me on this journey, and you will be with me through this journey as you are through all of my trials. Help me, Lord, to see you in everything I need to do and in everyone I need to hold up in prayer. Help me to accept where you have placed me and to trust in your perfect plan for my life. I turn it all over to you. Father, use me and mold me so I may be better equipped to see and serve you. In your holy name I pray. Amen and Amen.

TIME TO REFOCUS

Then Ananias went to the house and entered it. Placing his hands on Saul, he said, "Brother Saul, the Lord — Jesus, who appeared to you on the road as you were coming here — has sent me so that you may see again and be filled with the Holy Spirit." Immediately, something like scales fell from Saul's eyes, and he could see again. —ACTS 9:17 – 18

If you are unfamiliar with this story, allow me to set the stage. Saul (better known by his later name — Paul) was a man on a misguided mission to persecute followers of Jesus. The book of Acts records that Saul was "breathing out murderous threats against the Lord's disciples" (Acts 9:1), spending every waking minute searching for them to take them as prisoners ... until God zapped him with a blinding light on the road to Damascus. This encounter was intense. "For three days he was blind, and did not eat or drink anything" (Acts 9:9).

I have always been curious about the fact that Saul, now blind, sat for three days without eating or drinking. Naturally there was nothing he could do about the blindness; he was powerless to fix that problem. To be sure, God got Saul's attention in a rather dramatic way. But why did Saul stop eating and drinking? As I pondered that question, it occurred to me that the physical blindness Saul experienced was in a way a metaphor of the spiritual blindness of his heart. God wanted Saul to refocus his attention. And Saul had some heavy-duty issues to process without the distractions of food.

While I've never been blind, in some small way I understand how blurred vision can get your attention. After undergoing LASIK surgery, I enjoyed the convenience of sight without the hassle of contacts or glasses. For the first time in many years I didn't need glasses to see in the distance, nor did I require glasses for reading. In fact, my sight was actually slightly better than it was prior to the procedure, with the assistance of glasses.

About three years after I had the surgery, however, I had to return to the eye doctor because my vision was getting blurred and I was finding it difficult to maintain focus. Talk about an unsettling feeling. Reading, walking, driving — every aspect of my life was affected by the clouding of my vision. Thankfully, the doc reminded me that since the surgery my eyes no longer produce sufficient tears to keep my vision clear. Thanks to a bottle of "fake tears," I could see clearly again.

I realize there's a big difference between what Saul experienced with his blindness and my muddled vision. And yet in both cases God used something physical to get our attention. Why? Because ultimately our focus needs to be on him — not on our circumstances, and definitely not on what we think we ought to be doing with our lives. After all, Saul thought he was being zealous for God by persecuting Christians. He even made a career out of dragging them to jail. Talk about being way off track.

How about you? Has your vision of where you are in life become blurred? Has the stress of your transition journey caused you to feel that your faith just isn't working? Does it seem like nothing you're doing to correct the course of your career is working the way you had hoped? Is God using this season to help you refocus on him?

I believe our journey requires regular and frequent fine-tuning of our vision and continual reliance upon our relationship with the Lord. Just as I need to use that bottle of fake tears on a daily basis to maintain clear vision, you and I need to remain focused on the Lord and trust him to ensure a clear picture of where we should be going today and in the days ahead.

POINTS TO PONDER:

What has brought tears to your eyes during this journey? In what ways have you taken your eyes off of the Lord this week? What can you do to see God work in your life more clearly?

_____

_____

_____

_____

_____

_____

_____

_____

_____

_____

_____

_____

_____

_____

_____

_____

_____

_____

_____

_____

_____

HELP WANTED:

Lord Jesus, I pray for vision today — not that my eyes would see more clearly but that my heart would see more clearly. I long for the scales to fall from my eyes so that I can see with clarity your grand design for my life. I pray this in your holy name. Amen and Amen.

VERSES OF HOPE

Angels comfort people

Hebrews 1:14

Comforting others,

Esther 2:11
Job 6:14
Job 16:20 – 21
Job 42:11
Ecclesiastes 4:9 – 12
Song of Songs 8:7
Galatians 6:2
1 Thessalonians 2:12
1 Thessalonians 3:12
1 Thessalonians 4:16 – 18
Philemon 7
Hebrews 3:13
Hebrews 10:24,34
James 5:14,16
1 Peter 3:9
1 John 2:28
1 John 4:7

Fearful, God offers hope to the

Leviticus 26:6
Deuteronomy 31:6 – 8
1 Kings 1:29
2 Kings 6:16
Psalm 3:5 – 6
Psalm 16:8
Psalm 23:4
Psalm 27:1,3
Psalm 34:4
Psalm 46:1 – 3
Psalm 56:3 – 4,11
Psalm 91:5 – 7
Psalm 118:6

Proverbs 1:33
Proverbs 3:24 – 25
Isaiah 12:2
Isaiah 35:4
Isaiah 41:10,13
Isaiah 43:1 – 2,5
Isaiah 44:2
Isaiah 54:4
Jeremiah 1:8
Jeremiah 17:8
Lamentations 3:57
Ezekiel 34:28
Haggai 2:5
Matthew 10:28
Luke 12:6 – 7,32
John 14:27
Acts 18:9 – 10
Hebrews 13:6

Forgiveness, God offers hope with his

2 Chronicles 7:14
Psalm 32:5
Psalm 79:9
Psalm 103:1 – 4,12
Psalm 130:4
Isaiah 1:18
Isaiah 6:6 – 7
Isaiah 33:24
Isaiah 40:1 – 2
Isaiah 43:25
Isaiah 44:22
Isaiah 59:20
Ezekiel 18:23
Ezekiel 36:29 – 30,33
Micah 7:9,18
Zechariah 13:1
Mark 11:25

Acts 5:31
Acts 10:43
Acts 13:38 – 39
Acts 26:18
Romans 6:18
Romans 8:1
Ephesians 4:32
Colossians 2:13
Colossians 3:12 – 14
Hebrews 8:12
Hebrews 10:22
1 John 1:7
1 John 1:9

God offers hope to those who fear him

Psalm 37:16
Psalm 52:9
Psalm 58:11
Psalm 65:4
Psalm 71:21
Psalm 84:11
Psalm 92:12
Psalm 100:1 – 3
Psalm 128:1
Psalm 139:3 – 4,13 – 14,16,23
Psalm 140:13
Psalm 145:18 – 19
Psalm 147:11
Proverbs 2:21
Proverbs 12:2
Proverbs 14:26
Proverbs 19:23
Proverbs 21:21
Proverbs 28:25
Proverbs 29:25
Ecclesiastes 8:5
Isaiah 30:18
Isaiah 33:6
Isaiah 48:10 – 11
Isaiah 49:14 – 16
Isaiah 50:10

Isaiah 56:6 – 7
Isaiah 62:2
Isaiah 64:4
Isaiah 65:13
Jeremiah 1:5
Jeremiah 17:7
Jeremiah 24:7
Ezekiel 18:20
Daniel 12:3
Malachi 3:16
Malachi 4:2
Matthew 13:43
Matthew 19:29
Matthew 24:22
Matthew 25:21,34,46
Mark 3:35
Mark 8:35
Mark 9:41
Mark 10:29 – 30
Mark 11:23
Mark 12:42 – 43
Luke 10:20
John 1:12
John 9:31
John 12:26
John 14:1,12
John 15:2
Romans 2:10
Romans 8:28
Romans 9:33
Romans 10:11
1 Corinthians 1:8
1 Corinthians 2:9
1 Corinthians 8:3
2 Corinthians 7:9
Ephesians 6:8
1 Timothy 4:8
2 Timothy 2:19
1 Peter 2:5 – 6
1 John 3:22
Revelation 2:11 – 26,26

Revelation 3:4,21
Revelation 7:17
Revelation 14:13
Revelation 21:4,17

Guidance, God offers hope with his

Psalm 23:1 – 3
Psalm 25:5
Psalm 37:23
Psalm 48:14
Psalm 73:23 – 24
Proverbs 3:5 – 6
Proverbs 16:3
Isaiah 40:11
Isaiah 48:17
Isaiah 57:18
Isaiah 58:11
Jeremiah 29:11
Ezekiel 34:31
John 10:27
John 15:15

Healing and restoration, God offers hope with his

Isaiah 41:18 – 19
Isaiah 43:19
Isaiah 51:3
Isaiah 54:11
Isaiah 58:8
Isaiah 65:17,19
Jeremiah 29:12 – 14
Jeremiah 30:17
Jeremiah 31:28
Jeremiah 33:6
Ezekiel 11:19
Ezekiel 36:24 – 26
Amos 9:11,14 – 15
Zechariah 10:6
1 Corinthians 13:10
2 Corinthians 5:1,17

Joy, God offers hope with his

Job 1:21
Psalm 4:7
Psalm 30:5,11 – 12
Psalm 86:4
Psalm 97:11
Psalm 126:5 – 6
Ecclesiastes 5:19
Isaiah 35:10
Isaiah 51:3,11
Isaiah 52:9
Isaiah 54:1
Isaiah 61:7
Isaiah 65:14
Jeremiah 31:13
Habakkuk 3:17 – 18
John 15:11
John 16:22,24
Romans 12:12,15
1 Thessalonians 5:16 – 18
Jude 24 – 25

Listening, God comforts by

Psalm 4:3
Psalm 34:15,17
Psalm 38:15
Psalm 55:16 – 17
Psalm 102:17
Psalm 116:1 – 2
Psalm 138:3
Proverbs 15:29
Isaiah 30:19
Isaiah 59:1
Jeremiah 29:12 – 14
Lamentations 3:57
Micah 7:7
Zechariah 13:9
Matthew 7:7 – 8
Matthew 18:19
Mark 11:24
John 9:31

Acts 10:4,31
Hebrews 5:7
1 Peter 5:7

Love, God offers hope with his

Deuteronomy 10:14 – 15
1 Chronicles 16:34
Psalm 8:4
Psalm 13:5
Psalm 23:6
Psalm 25:10
Psalm 27:10
Psalm 31:7
Psalm 32:10
Psalm 33:18 – 19,22
Psalm 36:7 – 8
Psalm 37:28
Psalm 59:16
Psalm 86:15,17
Psalm 94:18 – 19
Psalm 106:1
Psalm 107:1
Psalm 116:5
Psalm 119:76
Psalm 130:7 – 8
Psalm 145:8 – 9
Proverbs 3:11 – 12
Isaiah 49:14 – 16
Jeremiah 31:2 – 3,20
Lamentations 3:19 – 22,31 – 33
Mark 10:21
John 14:23
Romans 2:4
Romans 5:8
Romans 8:35 – 39
Romans 12:21
1 Corinthians 13:13
Ephesians 3:17 – 19
Philippians 2:1 – 2
2 Thessalonians 2:16 – 17
2 Peter 3:9

1 John 4:7,17

Mercy, God offers hope with

Leviticus 26:5
Deuteronomy 4:31
Deuteronomy 30:3
2 Samuel 22:51
Nehemiah 9:31
Psalm 4:1
Psalm 6:2 – 4
Psalm 30:9 – 10
Psalm 57:1
Isaiah 12:1
Jeremiah 3:12
Jeremiah 18:8
Jeremiah 31:37
Micah 7:18,20
Luke 1:78 – 79
Romans 12:19 – 20
1 Timothy 1:16
Hebrews 4:16
1 Peter 2:10

Needy, God offers hope to the

Genesis 2:18a
Leviticus 26:10
Deuteronomy 10:18
1 Samuel 2:8
Psalm 9:18
Psalm 12:5
Psalm 30:2
Psalm 40:17
Psalm 68:6
Psalm 69:33
Psalm 70:5
Psalm 107:9
Psalm 109:21 – 22,31
Psalm 111:5
Psalm 113:7 – 8
Psalm 140:12
Psalm 146:7 – 9

Proverbs 10:3
Isaiah 29:19
Isaiah 41:17
Jeremiah 20:13
Luke 6:20 – 21
James 1:27
James 2:5

Peace, God offers hope with

Leviticus 26:6
Numbers 6:24 – 26
Judges 6:23 – 24
Psalm 29:11
Psalm 116:7
Proverbs 16:7
Ecclesiastes 4:6
Isaiah 26:3 – 4
Isaiah 32:17
Isaiah 54:10
Isaiah 55:12
Isaiah 57:2
Jeremiah 33:6
Ezekiel 34:25
Isaiah 66:12 – 13
John 14:27
John 16:33
Acts 9:31
Romans 5:1 – 2
Philippians 4:6 – 7
Philemon 3
2 John 3
3 John 14b

Power, God offers hope with his

Psalm 139:13 – 14
Ecclesiastes 11:5
Isaiah 33:21
Isaiah 40:10
Isaiah 55:8
Daniel 2:20 – 22
Zechariah 14:9

Matthew 19:26
Mark 10:26 – 27
Luke 21:27
John 9:1 – 3
Romans 8:28,31
2 Corinthians 12:9
Ephesians 6:10
Colossians 1:11
1 Thessalonians 3:13
2 Timothy 1:7
1 Peter 5:6

Presence, God offers hope with his

Genesis 8:1
Exodus 33:14,19
Deuteronomy 31:6 – 8
Joshua 1:9
Judges 6:12
1 Kings 8:27 – 31
Job 22:26
Psalm 11:7
Psalm 17:15
Psalm 22:9 – 11
Psalm 27:4 – 5,10
Psalm 46:10
Psalm 73:25
Psalm 95:7
Psalm 102:28
Psalm 116:15
Psalm 124:8
Psalm 125:1
Psalm 139:7 – 10,17 – 18
Isaiah 4:5
Isaiah 43:2
Isaiah 60:1 – 2
Isaiah 62:11
Jeremiah 30:22
Ezekiel 20:40 – 41
Ezekiel 34:30
Hosea 6:3
Jonah 2:2

Haggai 1:13
Haggai 2:4
Zechariah 1:3
Zechariah 2:10 – 13
Zechariah 8:23
Zechariah 13:9
Zechariah 14:9
Matthew 18:20
Matthew 28:20
Luke 21:27
Luke 23:43
John 14:3
John 14:18
John 16:32
Acts 1:11
Acts 17:27
Philippians 4:4 – 5
Hebrews 13:5
James 4:8
1 John 2:28
1 John 3:2
Revelation 11:12
Revelation 14:1
Revelation 21:3 – 5

Promises and faithfulness, God offers hope with his

Genesis 22:17
Genesis 28:15
Exodus 19:5 – 6
Leviticus 26:5
Deuteronomy 4:31
Deuteronomy 7:6,9
Deuteronomy 10:14 – 21
Deuteronomy 14:2
Deuteronomy 15:6
Deuteronomy 26:18
Deuteronomy 28:1
1 Samuel 12:22
1 Samuel 15:29
1 Kings 8:56

2 Chronicles 20:20
2 Chronicles 30:9
Psalm 9:10
Psalm 27:13
Psalm 31:23 – 24
Psalm 37:3 – 5
Psalm 37:7 – 9
Psalm 37:18
Psalm 37:34
Psalm 39:6 – 7
Psalm 71:5
Psalm 94:14
Psalm 111:5
Psalm 112:6
Psalm 119:50
Ecclesiastes 7:14
Isaiah 9:1,6
Isaiah 11:6
Isaiah 42:3
Isaiah 44:3
Isaiah 49:7
Isaiah 49:22
Isaiah 65:25
Isaiah 66:22
Jeremiah 23:5
Jeremiah 30:8 – 9
Jeremiah 31:8 – 9
Lamentations 3:23 – 24
Ezekiel 16:60
Ezekiel 34:25
Daniel 2:44
Daniel 7:27
Amos 9:13 – 15
Micah 2:12 – 13
Zechariah 3:7
Malachi 4:3
Matthew 8:11
Matthew 16:27
Matthew 25:34
Luke 18:29 – 30
Luke 22:30

Luke 23:43
John 13:36
John 14:2 – 3
Acts 1:11
1 Corinthians 1:9
1 Corinthians 6:2
2 Corinthians 1:20
2 Corinthians 7:1
Galatians 3:29
Galatians 6:9
Ephesians 6:8
Philippians 1:6
2 Thessalonians 1:6 – 7
Hebrews 6:10
Hebrews 10:23,36
Hebrews 11:1
Hebrews 13:5,13 – 14
James 1:12,25
1 Peter 5:4
2 Peter 1:4
2 Peter 3:9
Revelation 2:26
Revelation 11:18
Revelation 22:7,12

Protection, God offers hope with his

Genesis 15:1
Genesis 50:20
Exodus 14:14
Exodus 15:2
Exodus 23:22
Deuteronomy 20:4
Deuteronomy 32:10,43
Deuteronomy 33:12,27,29
Joshua 23:10
Ruth 2:13
1 Samuel 2:9
2 Samuel 22:1 – 7
2 Kings 17:39
2 Chronicles 14:11
Ezra 8:22

Psalm 3:2 – 3
Psalm 4:8
Psalm 5:12
Psalm 7:1
Psalm 9:9
Psalm 17:14
Psalm 18:1 – 6,16,30,46 – 49
Psalm 20:7
Psalm 22:19 – 21
Psalm 31:1 – 2,14 – 15
Psalm 32:6 – 7
Psalm 33:18 – 21
Psalm 34:7,17,22
Psalm 36:7 – 8
Psalm 40:1 – 2
Psalm 41:2
Psalm 44:6 – 7
Psalm 46:1
Psalm 50:15
Psalm 54:3 – 4
Psalm 59:9,16
Psalm 60:12
Psalm 61:4
Psalm 62:7 – 8
Psalm 63:6 – 8
Psalm 81:10
Psalm 91:1,3,9,11
Psalm 94:17,22
Psalm 97:10
Psalm 115:11
Psalm 118:17
Psalm 121:1 – 3,7 – 8
Psalm 135:14
Psalm 138:7
Psalm 144:2
Proverbs 3:26
Proverbs 14:32
Proverbs 18:10
Isaiah 4:6
Isaiah 11:9
Isaiah 41:11

Isaiah 43:2
Isaiah 52:12
Jeremiah 1:19
Jeremiah 15:15,20
Jeremiah 16:19
Jeremiah 20:11
Ezekiel 34:11
Daniel 12:1
Joel 3:16
Micah 5:4
Nahum 1:7
Luke 21:18
Acts 18:9 – 10
1 Corinthians 10:13
2 Thessalonians 3:3 – 5
Hebrews 2:16 – 18
2 Peter 2:9

Provision, God offers hope with his

Genesis 39:20 – 21
Psalm 34:9 – 10
Isaiah 33:16
Isaiah 55:1
Isaiah 66:11
Ezekiel 34:29
Ezekiel 36:11,29 – 30
Joel 2:19,25 – 26
Joel 3:18
Amos 9:13
Zechariah 10:1
Malachi 3:10,12
Matthew 6:8,31 – 34
Matthew 7:7 – 11
Luke 11:9 – 10
Luke 12:25 – 26,28
John 16:24
Romans 8:32
Romans 11:29
2 Corinthians 9:10 – 11
Philippians 4:12,19
Hebrews 11:16

James 1:5,17
1 John 3:22

Salvation, God offers hope with his

Exodus 15:2
Leviticus 26:13
Daniel 12:1
2 Samuel 7:24
Job 19:25 – 27
Psalm 19:14
Psalm 20:6
Psalm 22:3 – 5
Psalm 28:8
Psalm 35:9
Psalm 37:39
Psalm 49:15
Psalm 62:1 – 2
Psalm 71:14 – 15,20
Psalm 85:9
Psalm 91:3
Psalm 118:14
Psalm 138:7
Psalm 149:4
Isaiah 25:8 – 9
Isaiah 33:22
Isaiah 35:4
Isaiah 45:17,22
Isaiah 46:13
Isaiah 49:9
Isaiah 51:5
Isaiah 52:9
Isaiah 56:1
Isaiah 57:1
Isaiah 59:1
Isaiah 61:10
Jeremiah 17:14
Jeremiah 33:15 – 16
Ezekiel 34:22
Hosea 13:14
Joel 2:32
Obadiah 17

Habakkuk 3:17 – 18
Zephaniah 3:17
Matthew 24:22
Mark 13:13,27
Luke 3:17
Luke 20:36
Luke 21:28
Luke 22:29
John 3:15
John 3:16,36
John 4:14
John 5:24,29
John 6:39 – 40
John 8:12,51
John 10:10
John 11:25 – 26
John 12:25
John 17:2,22,24
Acts 20:32
Romans 2:7
Romans 5:1 – 2,8 – 9,17
Romans 6:22 – 23
Romans 8:11,16 – 17,32 – 34
Romans 10:9
Romans 13:11
Romans 14:9
Romans 16:20
1 Corinthians 3:21
1 Corinthians 15:52 – 57
2 Corinthians 4:14 – 15
2 Corinthians 5:1,21
2 Corinthians 8:9
Galatians 2:20
Galatians 3:26
Galatians 4:6 – 7
Galatians 5:1
Galatians 6:8
Ephesians 1:3 – 6,7 – 8,18
Ephesians 2:7 – 9
Philippians 1:21
Philippians 3:12,20

Colossians 1:5,12
Colossians 3:2 – 4,24
1 Thessalonians 4:16 – 18
1 Thessalonians 5:9
2 Thessalonians 2:13 – 14
2 Timothy 2:10
2 Timothy 4:8
Titus 2:11,14
Titus 3:7
Hebrews 2:14 – 15
Hebrews 7:25
Hebrews 9:15,28
Hebrews 12:2 – 3,22 – 23,28
1 Peter 1:2,3 – 5,8 – 9
1 Peter 2:9
2 Peter 1:10 – 11
2 Peter 2:9
1 John 2:17,25
1 John 5:4,13
1 John 5:13
Jude 24 – 25
Revelation 1:6
Revelation 2:7
Revelation 2:17
Revelation 3:5,10,12
Revelation 11:18
Revelation 20:4
Revelation 22:14

Spirit, God offers hope with his

Joel 2:28
Haggai 2:5
Acts 2:17
Acts 9:31
Romans 5:3 – 5
Romans 8:11,14 – 17,26
Romans 15:13
2 Corinthians 1:21 – 22
2 Corinthians 5:5
Philippians 2:1 – 2
Galatians 4:6 – 7

Suffering, God offers hope to those who are

Exodus 2:25
Exodus 3:7
Exodus 6:6
Psalm 10:17
Psalm 22:24
Psalm 25:16 – 17
Psalm 34:18
Psalm 42:5
Psalm 43:5
Psalm 51:17
Psalm 56:8
Psalm 68:19
Psalm 119:50,71
Psalm 147:3
Isaiah 49:13
Isaiah 50:7
Isaiah 53:3
Isaiah 57:15
Isaiah 61:1 – 2
Ezekiel 34:29
Matthew 5:3 – 4
Luke 16:22
Romans 5:3 – 5
Romans 8:18
Romans 12:15
2 Corinthians 1:3 – 5
2 Corinthians 4:17
2 Corinthians 7:6
2 Thessalonians 1:5
2 Timothy 1:12
2 Timothy 2:10
Hebrews 2:10
James 1:2 – 4
1 Peter 1:6 – 7
1 Peter 3:17
1 Peter 4:13
1 Peter 5:7 – 10
Revelation 2:10

Weak, God offers hope to the

Deuteronomy 32:36
Ruth 2:13
2 Chronicles 16:9
Nehemiah 8:10
Psalm 27:14
Psalm 28:7 – 8
Psalm 29:11
Psalm 41:1
Psalm 54:3 – 4
Psalm 55:22
Psalm 73:26
Psalm 145:14
Isaiah 40:28 – 31
Isaiah 46:4
Isaiah 60:22
Habakkuk 3:19
Zechariah 10:11 – 12
Matthew 5:3
Matthew 11:28 – 30
Matthew 18:10
Matthew 19:13 – 14
Luke 18:16
Romans 8:26
1 Corinthians 10:13
Philippians 4:13
Hebrews 2:16 – 18
Hebrews 4:15
Hebrews 5:2

Word, God offers hope with his

Psalm 119:7,105,114,147,165
Ecclesiastes 3:1
Isaiah 2:3
Isaiah 51:16
Isaiah 59:21
Matthew 4:4